What are Coincidences?

A Philosophical Guide Between Science and Common Sense

Alessandra Melas
University of Sassari, Italy

Pietro Salis
University of Cagliari, Italy

Series in Philosophy of Science

VERNON PRESS

In the Americas:
Vernon Press
1000 N West Street, Suite 1200,
Wilmington, Delaware 19801
United States

In the rest of the world:
Vernon Press
C/Sancti Espiritu 17,
Malaga, 29006
Spain

Series in Philosophy of Science

Library of Congress Control Number: 2023943645

ISBN: 978-1-64889-947-8

Also available: 978-1-64889-768-9 [Hardback]; 978-1-64889-794-8 [PDF, E-Book]

Cover image by Adriana Melas.

Table of Contents

List of Figures

Preface

Coincidences have been the focus of our collaborative side-project for quite some time. To be more precise, this book is the outcome of our shared research work on the nature of coincidences in the last ten years. During our collaboration, we have been presenting our ideas on coincidences in many international conferences, especially during the years 2013-2016. We presented parts of our work on coincidences in the following venues: at the SIFA (Italian Society for Analytic Philosophy) Graduate Conference 2013, University of Cagliari (Italy); at the SIFA 2014 Conference, University of L'Aquila (Italy); at the PSSA (Philosophical Society of South Africa) 2015 Conference, Nelson Mandela Metropolitan University (Port Elizabeth, South Africa); at the GAP.9 conference of the German Society for Analytic Philosophy in 2015, University of Osnabrück (Germany); and at the SIFA 2016 Conference, University of Florence (Pistoia Uniser Campus, Italy). We are thankful to all the audiences who attended our presentations for all the comments and suggestions that we succeeded to collect on those occasions and that greatly helped us improve our work.

Although we have been doing research on coincidences for years and have been so far mainly focused on publishing some articles in peer reviewed journals, we thought about putting our published papers together with new materials in order to provide readers with a thorough and more accessible presentation of our views.[1] On top of that, this book mainly represents an expansion of our work in new directions and with a special focus on recent literature on coincidences. We especially expanded our previous work in three different directions: first of all, by highlighting the contribution of the main historical antecedents of this research, focusing especially on the work of Antoine Augustine Cournot and Jacques Monod; second, by addressing the current rival approach in the philosophical understanding of coincidences, which has recently become the so-called "common cause" view, defended by Tamar Lando; and finally, by exploring new materials coming from cognitive psychology—especially the work of cognitive scientists Mark K. Johansen and Magda Osman—that can be in principle understood

---

[1] Our articles are the following: Alessandra Melas, "Cournot's Notion of Hasard: an Objective Conception of Chance", *Axiomathes* 27, no. 6 (2017):685, https://doi.org/10.1007/s10516-017-9333-7; Alessandra Melas and Pietro Salis, "On the Nature of Coincidental Events", *Axiomathes* 32, no. 1 (2022):143, https://doi.org/10.1007/s10516-020-09517-4

as a brand new benchmark to evaluate virtues and flaws of the main views on coincidences under scrutiny.

The article "Cournot's Notion of Hasard: An Objective Conception of Chance" has been widened here to be part of Chapter 2. The article "On the Nature of Coincidental Events" has been divided in two parts: the introductory section has been inserted in the introduction as we found particularly useful the general presentation of the philosophical problem of coincidences that it contained, so that we could expand it to the whole book; the other sections of that article compose Chapter 4 of this book. Chapter 3 and Chapter 5 contain new and previously unpublished materials. Finally, in Chapter 2, the parts concerning Monod's views are new and previously unpublished. Though the book is the outcome of a common, shared effort, Alessandra Melas is mainly responsible for Chapter 2 and Chapter 5, while Pietro Salis is mainly responsible for Chapter 3. In Chapter 1, Alessandra Melas is mainly responsible for the section "An intersection of independent causal lines", while Pietro Salis is mainly responsible for the sections "Going beyond the tradition", "Open problems" and "Plan of the book". In Chapter 4, Alessandra Melas is mainly responsible for the sections "Beyond intersectionism", "The ontic dimension: Are there intersections between truly independent causal sequences? Some degrees of causal independence", "Probability", and "Control", while Pietro Salis is mainly responsible for the sections "The epistemic dimension: are coincidences mind-dependent?", "The role of epistemic access", "The degree of epistemic access", "Collateral aspects of the epistemic dimension", "Attitudes and beliefs", and "Conclusion".

Alessandra Melas would like to thank her master, Professor Alberto Mario Mura, for having introduced her to the challenging and intriguing world of coincidences, as well as Dr. Bernard D. Beitman and his Coincidence Research Group for the helpful discussions. She would also like to thank all her friends, especially Alina, Anna, Daniela, Gesy, Giovanna, Irene, Roberta, Nina, Albino, Luca and Mario, and her family for their precious support.

Pietro Salis would like to thank his partner Gianfranca and his family for their priceless support. He would also like to thank all his colleagues at the Department of Education, Psychology and Philosophy of the University of Cagliari, for providing an especially stimulating and collaborative environment.

Alghero and Cagliari, December 20th 2022

Chapter 1
Introduction

An Intersection of Independent Causal Lines

Usually, chance is illustrated as a special region of the physical world, one in which the usual causal explanations find interesting application limits. In fact, the specialness of chance events is that they show a structural tendency to evade and/or resist causal explanation. A subclass of chance events[1] of particular interest is that called "coincidences". According to the prevailing view in the philosophical tradition, coincidences are events that come from the intersections between independent causal chains. One example, provided by David Owens, is an accidental collision between a person sitting in a particular place and a falling cargo door:

> It is a coincidence that I was sitting at the spot where the cargo door fell—this event can be analysed into two events (a) my sitting at place A and (b) the cargo door's landing at place A, events which have quite independent causal histories [...].[2]

One of the leading views regarding chance in the tradition is provided, for the very first time in modern age, by French philosopher Antoine-Augustin Cournot. As he highlights, the core of this conception of chance consists of the mutual independence of the intersecting causal chains:

> It is necessary, to be more precise, to focus exclusively on what is fundamental and categorical in the notion of chance, namely, the idea of independence or non-solidarity among various series of causes [...].[3]

---

[1] This work does not engage in a metaphysical discussion on the distinction between processes, events, properties, times, and so on. However, we take it for granted that coincidences are events and not properties. Though coincidences are hybrids, that is composed entities, they are individuals, since they are not construed as universals. The difference between individuals and properties lies in the fact that individuals are singularities while properties "recur". Since coincidences are rare entities, they cannot be treated as recurrent and universal properties. Chapter 4 explains why we think that coincidences are hybrids.

[2] David Owens, *Causes and Coincidences* (Oxford: Oxford University Press, 1992), 12.

[3] Antoine Augustine Cournot, *Essai sur les Fondements de nos Connaissances et sur les Caractères de la Critique Philosophique* (Paris: Hachette, 1851), 56, the italics are ours. The

Therefore, according to Cournot's view, coincidental events are strictly defined as the result of intersections between independent causal lines. The examples provided thus far consider causal intersections as causal interactions, and this is what we want to do in this book: when we talk about "intersecting causal lines" we are talking about some kind of physical interaction in space and time between causal processes, even though—as we are going to see—not all intersections are like this.

This view about causal intersections in the understanding of coincidences has gained and is going to gain further centrality in the philosophical tradition more in general, as the following relevant quotation from Cournot shows very well:

> Those events brought by the combination or the meeting of other events that belong to mutual independent series, are what we consider fortuitous events, or the result of chance.[4]

As anticipated, Cournot is not alone in defending such a causal view about coincidences. In fact, this genus of causal view of chance is also defended one century later by Cournot's more famous compatriot Jacques Monod, a biologist Nobel Prize winner who was also a philosopher:

> [...] Such is the case, for instance, in what may be called "absolute coincidences", those, that is to say, which result from the intersection of two totally independent chains of events.[5]

However, it is important to remark that coincidences—though they are events that can be understood in causal terms—cannot be explained in causal terms: we are able to say that they come from the intersection between independent causal chains, but we are not able to explain why that intersection happens. So that, coincidences are—in some sense—unexplainable events, in line with what some literature says. With "chance", in fact, the concerning literature

---

original passage in French is as follows: «Il faut, pour bien s'entendre, s'attacher exclusivement à ce qu'il y a de fondamental et de catégorique dans la notion du hasard, savoir, à l'idée de l'indépendance ou de la non-solidarité entre diverses séries de causes [...]».

[4] Cournot, *Essai sur les Fondements de nos Connaissances et sur les Caractères de la Critique Philosophique*, 52. The original passage in French is as follows: «Les évènements amenés par la combinaison ou la rencontre d'autres évènements qui appartiennent à des séries indépendantes les unes des autres, sont ce qu'on nomme des évènements fortuits, ou des résultats du hasard».

[5] Jacques Monod, *Chance and Necessity: Essay on the Natural Philosophy of Modern Biology* (New York: Vintage, 1971), 114.

indicates something that cannot be causally explained,[6] and the same can be said for coincidences. So that, an event is chance or coincidental if:

- it occurs without a definite and identifiable cause, i.e., contradicting the Principle of Causality that assigns a precise cause to every event.

- it has happened for causes that are certainly there but are non-linear, i.e., causes may cross in a non-predictable and non-understandable way.

This last case illustrates well why coincidences are usually taken to be unexplainable events.[7] The inexplicability of coincidences is exactly represented in terms of the mutual independence between the causal lines involved. Since the involved causal chains have independent causal histories, to explain each individual causal line is not the same as to explain the intersection between the involved lines. In this context, an explanation is conceived as something that cannot be reduced to laws and background conditions. This is because laws are common to law-like phenomena and accidents. As in Owens' example, all of the cargo doors falling down fall according to gravitational forces, but there is no law of nature according to which a particular cargo door must fall in that way and on that particular occasion. In the example of the cargo door accident, explaining the behaviour of every single intersecting causal process is ultimately insufficient to understand why the accident happened:

> To explain each of the parts of an event is not necessarily to explain the whole event. To explain the whole we must show that its parts share a

---

[6] As Wesley Salmon maintains, following a conception that seems to go back at least to Aristotle, "to give scientific explanation" is to show how "events [...] fit into the causal structure of the world". See Wesley Salmon, *Scientific Explanation and the Causal Structure of the World* (Princeton: Princeton University Press, 1984), 162. So that, if it is not possible to provide to an event a causal explanation, then that event must be considered chance.

[7] The relation between coincidence and explanation can be extended in principle to a very large number of cases. In particular, many issues rise in connection with the passage from physical to biological explanation. This is surely an interesting and challenging terrain for the approach we are defending here. Nonetheless, it requires much more space and specific work to be done, especially given the fact that the already complex debate is undergoing a recent twist due to issues concerning the notion of "emergence" and the concept of "delegated causality". See, for example, Raimundas Vidunas, "Delegated Causality of Complex Systems", *Axiomathes* 29, no. 1 (2019): 81; doi: https://doi.org/10.1007/s105 16-018-9377-3.

common cause, however complex and heterogeneous the elements of that common cause may be.[8]

To better clarify this point, let us consider the following example. Miss Anna and Miss Julia, two strangers from the same university, travel to the far side of the world and end up sitting at the neighbouring tables, in the same café at exactly the same time.

In this case, it is possible to explain why Miss Anna and Miss Julia are going to visit that café, as events considered in isolation, but—since the causal lines involved are independent from each other given the fact the Miss Anna has reasons to go there which are quite different from those ones which bring Julia in the same place, and given the fact they do not know each other's intentions—it is not possible to explain the intersection between Miss Anna's trajectory and Miss Julia's one. The independence of the relevant causal lines once again prevents us from having a plausible causal explanation of what is taking place in the example.

To sum up, coincidences are events that can be understood in causal terms, since they come from the intersection between independent causal histories, but they are—at the same time—events that cannot be explained in causal terms, given the independence between the causal chains involved.[9] In any case, the independence between the causal lines plays a crucial role in order to understand what coincidences are. With this remark, we connect to the fundamental philosophical distinction between explanation and description. According to this distinction, explanation concerns something—the explanandum—to be explained in terms of something else—the explanans—and this is mostly meant to be the spelling out of some causal relation or mechanism, hence what is caused is explained in terms of its proper cause; a significant variant of explanation works instead in terms of postulation, where certain imperceptible processes or entities—e.g., subatomic particles—are postulated in order to explain certain perceptible events—e.g., certain features or behaviours of physical objects; describing, to the contrary, works by connecting many types of information independently of how they are explained, and by trying to give

---

[8] Owens, *Causes and Coincidences*, 13.

[9] An interesting view concerning this point is provided by Tamar Lando. According to that conception, coincidences could share a common cause, but in that case they still fail to be explained: the two independent causal lines can issue from a common cause without an adequate explanation for the relational fact (in our example: the meeting of Miss Anna and Miss Julia). Lando's view, separating causation and causal explanation, states that not every common cause is an explanatory common cause. For a more detailed account of this approach, see Tamar Lando, "Coincidence and Common Cause", *Noûs* 51, no. 1 (2017): 132; doi: 10.1111/nous.12166 and chapter 3 of this book.

meaning to this ensemble. So philosophical theories try to describe what coincidences are since we cannot achieve a scientific (causal) explanation of them. In this sense, this is an investigation which concerns certain interesting limits of causal explanation, especially those connected with causal intersections.

However, someone may object that not every event that comes from the intersection between independent causal lines is a coincidence. What if, for example, Miss Anna and Miss Julia travel to the far side of the world and end up sitting at the neighbouring tables, in the same café at exactly the same time, but do not come from the same university? The independence between the intersecting causal lines is still there, but no trace of any coincidence. In that case, a good question could be the following: Is the independence between the intersecting causal lines sufficient to say that an event is a coincidence? It will soon be clear that our answer to this question is in the negative. A significant part of this study is devoted to explaining why.

Going Beyond the Tradition

Our basic approach to coincidences, on the one hand, is surely faithful to the tradition sketched so far, and accordingly acknowledges the view that coincidences are, in a fundamental sense, determined by the intersection of independent causal transitions. On the other hand, we plan to take into account certain features of coincidences that intuitively go beyond this merely causal approach. In particular, and with this we get for the first time to our point, coincidences are *interesting* for us, and such interest seems to rely on what we believe, on what we know, and on what we find in many ways significant. Hence, we think that epistemic and psychological aspects of agents and epistemic subjects are relevant parts of what is going on in coincidental events. This book will try to provide some convincing examples of these special features, since they do not reduce to causal intersections. However, this view is not entirely new and, as we are going to see soon, there is an important antecedent coming from a minority tradition about chance and coincidences that started in the philosophy of law. But let us start from the basics.

According to Achille Varzi, it is possible to fruitfully distinguish between ontology and metaphysics, even though they are often conflated in a systematic way: ontology is—very generally—the philosophical investigation about *what there is*; to the contrary, metaphysics deals with the more speculative question about the deep, or ultimate, *nature* of what there is.[10] Following Varzi's distinction, we could say that coincidences are constituted not only by the ontic

---

[10] Achille Varzi, *Ontologia* (Roma-Bari: Laterza, 2005), 7-18.

intersection[11] between independent causal chains but also, metaphysically, by certain epistemic and psychological conditions. One of the main goals of this book is to defend the idea that the epistemic and psychological aspects of coincidences are constitutive parts of coincidental phenomena.

As anticipated, this view was stated for the first time by Herbert Lionel Adolphus Hart and Antony Maurice Honoré, who said—in their *Causation in the Law*—that coincidences, as well as the fact that they come from the intersection of independent causal lines, (a) are events that are very unlikely by ordinary standards, (b) for some reason are significant or important, and (c) occur without any human contrivance.[12] Starting from Hart and Honoré's idea, in this book we develop a new account on the nature of coincidences, according to which coincidental events are—metaphysically speaking—hybrids constituted by ontic and epistemic/psychological components. Accordingly, we point out the insufficiency of a pure objectivist view of coincidences and of a purely object-oriented approach: this basically means that while we accept the traditional view, i.e., that the intersection of independent causal lines is undoubtedly necessary for coincidences, we think that this is not sufficient to provide a complete and satisfying understanding of coincidences.

However, in agreement with the traditional view, we state that the physical intersections between causal lines are surely mind independent. Whereas the acknowledgement of the independence between the intersecting causal lines that one can achieve is not mind independent, and furthermore, it even adds, together with certain mental aspects of the subject performing the acknowledgment,[13] new features to the same intersections. These new features are epistemic and psychological—and indeed mental—characteristics, and although they do not belong to the ontic dimension of the intersection, they show up in the relevant metaphysical account of coincidences. Hence, we take a position against a kind of "reductionism", according to which coincidences can be reduced to mere intersections between independent causal chains. Therefore, our conception—in line with Hart and Honoré's position—is a kind of hybrid

---

[11] By ontic intersections we mean intersections which happen in the actual world in a mind-independent way. Ontic intersections are objective in this specific manner: their objective realization does not depend on human epistemic states, intentions, and actions. Pay attention to the possible conflation between the notion of ontic intersections and the supposed conception of ontic coincidences. As will be clearer through this book, we deny the existence of ontic coincidences: ontic intersections do not suffice to yield coincidences.

[12] Herbert Lionel Adolphus Hart and Antony Maurice Honoré, *Causation in the Law* (Oxford: Clarendon Press, 1959), 74.

[13] See below for a taxonomy of these non-ontic features, which we address in Chapter 4.

and non-reductionist view, where coincidences are understood as rooted in different elements.

Finally, when we affirm that the mental and epistemic features of coincidences are non-ontic components, we are not advancing any anti-naturalistic view about the mind and/or knowledge: we are just sticking to the facts about available and tenable explanations; we do not have any purely causal explanation of mental states and epistemic states, and we know about many long-standing difficulties concerning these problematic attempts at explaining contentful states in causal terms.[14]

Open Problems

Our account of coincidences does not extend to certain related problems which are particularly controversial in current philosophical debates, especially those involved in the metaphysics of causation. We limit ourselves to the use of certain concepts given in the literature such as "events", when talking about causal intersections, because we are aware of the complications involving any other candidate concepts, such as "facts", "properties", "variable values" and the like.[15] This choice is at least useful to connect with the existing literature and in systematically avoiding to deal, at the current stage, with potentially incompatible frameworks and terminologies, as we easily avoid a number of conflations and equivocations. Not all these issues are that easy, however. There are certain open problems that will structurally constitute a crucial challenge for accounts like ours in the future, and depend on other, non-terminological, issues connected with our talk of causal intersections.

In fact, the recent literature concerning the metaphysics of causation has pointed out the causal relevance of omissions and absences in many genuine transitions.[16] As J. Dmitri Gallow nicely writes:

---

[14] See for example Wilfrid Sellars, *Empiricism and the Philosophy of Mind* (Cambridge MA: Harvard University Press, 1997[1956]); Daniel Hutto and Erik Myin, *Radicalizing Enactivism. Basic Minds without Contents* (Cambridge MA: The MIT Press, 2013), chap. 4.

[15] See J. Dmitri Gallow "The Metaphysics of Causation", *The Stanford Encyclopedia of Philosophy*, 2022, https://plato.stanford.edu/entries/causation-metaphysics/#Even.

[16] Helen Beebee, "Causing and Nothingness", in *Causation and Counterfactuals*, ed. John Collins, Ned Hall, and Laurie A. Paul (Cambridge, MA: MIT Press, 2004): 291; David M. Armstrong, *A World of States of Affairs* (Cambridge: Cambridge University Press, 1997); Judith Jarvis Thomson, "Causation: Omissions", *Philosophy and Phenomenological Research* 66, no. 1 (2003): 81; doi:10.1111/j.1933-1592.2003.tb00244.x; Michael S. Moore, *Causation and Responsibility: An Essay in Law, Morals, and Metaphysics* (Oxford: Oxford University Press, 2009), doi:10.1093/acprof:oso/9780199256860.001.0001.

[...], Anna's failure to water her plant may cause it to die. Here, we have an absence as a token cause. Likewise, Anna's vacation may have caused her to not water the plant. Here, we have an absence as a token effect. But it does not seem that absences or omissions are events. They are *nothings*, non-occurrences, and are hence not identical to any occurrent events.[17]

Examples like this clearly point out that there are problems with this loose talk about causal intersections as events. The case for the causal role of absences and omissions requires, in principle, some proper treatment, and the cases involving such occurrences are clearly problematic for the current use of "events" that we are making in this book. The concept of "event", or any surrogate concept that we may exploit in its stead, must be necessarily regimented or engineered in the future in order to satisfactorily handle such troublesome entailments.

The concept of "ontic intersection", as well, is clearly exposed to potential troublesome revisions. Omissions and absences, in principle, can be part of the transitions that we label causal intersections, but their "ontic" status is not certainly clear as it should. So, this will systematically be a dimension of expansion (or of revision) of a work like this. This also means that there is a tight connection between this investigation on chance and coincidences and what is going on in the more recent literature on the metaphysics of causation. Even though the debate is very rich in contributions and suggestions, we are at the moment not fully satisfied with what the debate has to offer, and especially with certain metaphysical implications concerning putative negative facts, negative properties, and the like: all the attempts at understanding omissions and absences in terms of some kind of negative facts do not strike us as particularly compelling.[18] We tend to think about such implications as basically in tension with our metaphysical preferences, and so would let the issue stay open for now, with the hope to be able, one day, to satisfactorily treat absences and omissions without the need to endorse or exploit naturalistically suspicious facts and properties.

---

[17] Gallow, "The Metaphysics of Causation", cit.

[18] We would, in principle, agree with Hart and Honoré that it is better to talk about negative statements as expressive of contrasts and comparisons (that is, as playing a pragmatic function), without the need to involve negative facts and properties (and the metaphysical puzzles which are likely to follow). We need more research in order to gain full confidence about the general feasibility of this intuitive idea. But if we would need to put a bet on this issue, our bucks would surely go to this option.

Plan of the Book

The second chapter of the book illustrates and analyses the causal conception of chance and coincidences provided by central authors such as Cournot and Monod, who as we saw have been the pioneering figures in setting up all the main theoretical issues. This is the principal philosophical tradition about understanding coincidences, and one that is especially concerned about the role played by causation in coincidental phenomena. This idea, as already anticipated, heavily revolves around the concept of "causal intersection": the idea that coincidences depend on independent causal chains that somehow intersect with each other in a given time. The chapter explores the theoretical pillars and the main contributions coming from this intersectionist tradition. Many examples are introduced and discussed throughout the chapter in order to provide a clear understanding of this causal view, which is needed as the necessary starting point for the following discussions.

The third chapter explores a completely different option by analysing an interesting contender to the principal intersectionist tradition about coincidences introduced in the second chapter. It is the view that coincidences are not always determined by the intersection of independent causal lines, but at least sometimes are determined by some common cause. An influential pioneer of this view has been the great German positivist philosopher of science, and founder of the Berlin Circle, Hans Reichenbach. In more recent times, a similar view has been defended and renewed by Tamar Lando, who provided an entirely new theoretical perspective and some new examples. Lando shows putative examples of coincidences which are not determined by independent causal lines, but which are determined by a common cause. If Lando is right, it follows that the understanding of coincidences as the outcomes of intersections between independent causal lines, i.e., traditional intersectionism, is a mistaken view. Hence, Lando's account is purported to challenge the tradition by means of the provision of fundamental counterexamples to it. We analyse Lando's proposal and discuss her examples in this chapter, in which we try to defend traditional intersectionism—which is one of the two main pillars of our wider understanding of coincidences. We try to defend intersectionism from Lando's attack and to offer alternative readings of Lando's examples which are basically in line with the intersectionist tradition.

The fourth chapter is a thorough presentation of our hybrid view about coincidences. As anticipated, we try to widen the traditional view of coincidences—that is the idea that coincidences are determined by the intersection of independent causal lines—by adding an analysis of other epistemic and psychological components which are, according to our intuitions, relevant for a philosophical understanding of coincidences. According to this view, meanings, beliefs and other attitudes play a crucial role, together with causal intersections, in determining what coincidences are. As stated, Hart and Honoré have been the first philosophers to promote and defend an approach of this kind in the debate. We defend the same hybrid view, but we exploit arguments and examples which are basically new, in order to provide new oxygen to this perspective. As a matter of fact, we try to characterize more in detail the role of epistemological and psychological components in determining coincidences, and we also try to explore some interesting interactions, relations and hierarchies among them. This analysis will permit us to highlight an entire list of relevant features and/or conditions for coincidental events that are crucial in understanding them as much as causal intersections.

The fifth chapter is more experimental in nature, since it aims at exploiting experiments and empirical data coming from psychological research concerning judgments about coincidences. Our main hypothesis is that such research would provide independent evidence for the important role that we assign to the psychological and epistemic aspects of coincidences. If these empirical findings are in line with our ideas and with our expectations, our view will gain relevant empirical support. Indeed, this would be the kind of evidence we need in order to defend our hybrid view where some psychological phenomenon is at work in determining coincidences. As we will see, the research work developed over the years by cognitive scientists Mark Johansen and Magda Osman is of crucial importance here, as they based their experiments on a definition of coincidences that we deem very close to ours.[19] Not only they fully vindicated, from an empirical point of view, the importance of the psychological aspects of coincidences, but they also highlighted how the main feature that we can notice from empirical experiments on "coincidence judgment" is a kind of "surprise effect" that systematically accompanies our experience with coincidences. This surprise effect, very interestingly, relates to a peculiar cognitive mechanism that is devoted to causally explain what goes on around us: if something happens that is both unlikely by chance and however the fruit of chance since we are unable to provide causal explanations for it, then we find the event (surprisingly) coincidental.

---

[19] According to them, coincidences are events which are made of "surprising pattern repetitions" that are observed to be almost unlikely by ordinary standards but are nonetheless attributed to chance because our regular attempts at causal explanation have not produced anything more plausible than "mere chance" (see Mark K. Johansen and Magda Osman, "Coincidences: A Fundamental Consequence of Rational Cognition", *New Ideas in Psychology* 39 (2015): 36, https://doi.org/10.1016/j.newideapsych.2015.07.001). For their experimental work see Mark K. Johansen and Magda Osman, "Coincidental Judgment in Causal Reasoning: How Coincidental is This?", *Cognitive Psychology* 120 (2020): 101290, https://doi.org/10.1016/j.cogpsych.2020.101290.

Chapter 2

Cournot, Monod, and the Causal

Cause and Coincidences

Let us start our discussion telling you three different stories concerning coincidences:

STORY 1:

"It was a very springy day and I decided to take a walk in the city centre, where everyone can see colourful balconies of red tulips and yellow daisies. But a tragedy was going to happen: a vase of red tulips fell before my eyes, hitting the head of the man who was walking just few metres ahead. The red of the tulip and the red of his blood mingled like in a huge reddish river. Such a bad luck! Such a terrible coincidence!".

STORY 2:

"Few weeks ago, I was watching a TV program on Boris Pasternak. Meanwhile, without knowing what I was doing, my best friend (who lives in Germany) was reading Doctor Zhivago. I called him the same evening and we realized that a couple of hours before we were both doing something that concerns Boris Pasternak. We have been friends since forever and it was like if we had telepathy! It was a coincidence that at the same time (but in different places) my friend and I were doing something that concerns Boris Pasternak".

STORY 3:

"I was in Prague with a friend; we went out to visit the city. After walking for miles, I decided to sit on one of the 1.000.000 benches that are in Prague. My friend took a photo with me sitting on that bench. I came back home, and I showed that photo to my mum, who displayed me a photo which, ten years before, my dad took with her sitting on the exact same bench! It was a shocking coincidence that my mum and I were sitting in the same place (but at different times) in Prague".

As we could read from the coincidence stories, to get a coincidence, there must be various elements: 1) there must be an element of surprise (Wow! What a coincidence!), 2) there must be an incidence of some things in space and time, 3) there must be the feeling that what happened had a very small probability to happen, but it did anyway, 4) the events which are involved in a coincidence must be seen as meaningfully related, such as in the case of Pasternak's story, and also the case of the bench's photograph.

Concerning point 2), which is the one we are engaging in a discussion about in this chapter, we get coincidences of different types.

1. Suppose that, like in the vase story, we have an incidence of some things (in that specific case an incidence between the tulips' falling vase and the man walking on the street) at the same time and at the same space, in a way that there is a match both in space and time. Let us call that "space/time-coincidence".

2. Differently, suppose that—like in Pasternak's story—we have an incidence of some things (in that specific case an incidence between my friend reading Pasternak's Doctor Zhivago and me watching a TV program on Boris Pasternak) at the same time, but in different spaces, in a way that there is a match in time, but not in space. This is a "time-coincidence".

3. Now, suppose that—like in the bench's photo story—we have an incidence of some things (in that specific case an incidence between me being photographed in a certain bench in Prague and my mum being photographed in the same exact bench in Prague much earlier) in the same place, but at different times, in a way that there is a match in space, but not in time. Let's call that "space-coincidence".

To sum up, it seems there are space/time-coincidences, time-coincidences, and space-coincidences. So that we have at least three kinds of coincidences.

What this chapter is trying to do consists in analysing coincidences of the first type, and then understanding more in depth the point 2) of the four elements quoted above.

Now a compelling question is: Where does this space/time idea of coincidences come from? At first sight, we can for sure say that it is very common in the natural sciences. But let us investigate it more carefully going back to its origins.

At the Origin of the Space/Time Coincidence View

In *Le Hasard et La Nécessité* Monod starting from the view—which someone ascribes to Democritus—that everything existing in the Universe is the fruit of chance and necessity, maintains that each alteration in the DNA happens by chance. Hence, chance—according to Monod—is the origin of every novelty happening in the biosphere, and then the driving force of evolution.

But which conception of chance is Monod talking about? According to Monod, chance events are the result of the intersection in space and time between different processes that belong to independent causal chains; intersections he calls "absolute coincidences".

The coincidental conception of chance is closely related to the Principle of Causality—according to which whatever comes to exist has a cause, conversely to a view which states that chance events are what cannot be described in causal terms. One of the main supporters of this view is David Hume, who—in his *Treatise of Human Nature*—says:

> There is but one kind of necessity, as there is but one kind of cause, and that the common distinction betwixt moral and physical necessity is without any fundamental nature. [...] 'Tis the constant conjunction of objects, along with the determination of the mind, which constitutes a physical necessity: and the removal of these is the same thing with chance. As objects must either be conjoin'd or not, and as the mind must either be determin'd or not to pass from one object to another, 'tis impossible to admit of any medium betwixt chance and an absolute necessity.[1]

Differently, according to a causal view of chance, chance events are simply the result of intersecting causal lines:

> [...] Such is the case, for instance, in what may be called "absolute coincidences", those, that is to say, which result from the intersection of two totally independent chains of events.[2]

This conception is illustrated in the following Monod's example: Dr. Dupont will be seeing a patient for the first time. Meanwhile, Mr. Dubois is repairing a roof in the same area. When Dr. Dupont comes across Mr. Dubois' workplace, Mr. Dubois inadvertently drops his hammer and the hammer's path intersects with Dr. Dupont's path, and he dies.[3]

---

[1] David Hume, *Treatise of Human Nature*, Book I, part III, section XIV (Oxford: Clarendon Press, 1888 [1739-40]).

[2] Monod, *Chance and Necessity*, 114. The original passage in French is as follows: «C'est le cas, par exemple, de ce que l'on peut appeler les "coïncidences absolues", c'est-à-dire celles qui résultent de l'intersection de deux chaînes causales totalement indépendantes l'une de l'autre» [1970].

[3] *Ibid.* From the original passage in French: «Supposons par exemple que le Dr. Dupont soit appelé d'urgence à visiter un nouveau malade, tandis que le plombier Dubois travaille à la réparation urgente de la toiture d'un immeuble voisin. Lorsque le Dr. Dupont passe au pied de l'immeuble, le plombier lâche par inadvertance son marteau, dont la trajectoire (déterministe) se trouve intercepter celle du médecin, qui en meurt le crâne fracassé» [1970].

Almost the same view can be found in Henri Poincaré:

> A man passes in the street on his way to his business; someone who knew about these affairs could say why he left at such a time, why he went through such a street. On the roof works a roofer; the entrepreneur who employs him will be able, to a certain extent, to foresee what he is going to do. But the man hardly thinks of the roofer, nor the roofer of the man: they seem to belong to two completely foreign worlds. And yet, the roofer drops a tile that kills the man, and we will not hesitate to say that this is a coincidence.[4]

And even before in Antoine Augustine Cournot, who says that:

> Those events brought by the combination or the meeting of other events that belong to mutual independent series, are what we consider fortuitous events, or the result of chance.[5]

A similar conception of chance can be also observed in Jean la Placette:

> I am persuaded that chance contains something real and positive, namely a concurrence of two or more contingent events, each of which has its causes, but in such a way that their concurrence has none except the we know. I am very mistaken if this is not what we mean when we speak of chance.[6]

---

[4] Henri Poincaré, *Calcul des Probabilités* (Paris: Gauthier-Villars, Imprimeur-Libraire, 1912), 10-11. The translation is ours. The original passage in French is as follows: «Un homme passe dans la rue en allant à ses affaires; quelqu'un qui aurait été au courant de ces affaires pourrait dire pour quelle raison il est parti à telle heure, pourquoi il est passé par telle rue. Sur le toit travaille un couvreur; l'entrepreneur qui l'emploie pourra, dans une certaine mesure, prévoir ce qu'il va faire. Mais l'homme ne pense guère au couvreur, ni le couvreur à l'homme: ils semblent appartenir a deux mondes complètement étrangers l'un à l'autre. Et pourtant, le couvreur laisse tomber une tuile qui tue l'homme, et on n'hésitera pas à dire que c'est là un hasard».

[5] Cournot, *Essai sur les Fondements de nos Connaissances et sur les Caractères de la Critique Philosophique*, 52. The translation is ours. The original passage in French is as follows: «Les événements amenés par la combinaison ou la rencontre d'autres événements qui appartiennent à des séries indépendantes les unes des autres, sont ce qu'on nomme des événements fortuits, ou des résultats du hasard».

[6] Jean la Placette, *Traité des jeux de hasard, défendus contre les objections de M. de Joncourt et de quelques autres* (La Haye: Chez Henry Scheurleer, Marchand Libraire prés de la Cour, à l'Enfeigne d'Erafme, 1714), 7. The translation is ours. The original passage in French is as follows: «Pour moi, je suis persuadé que le hasard renferme quelque chose de réel et de positif, savoir, un concours de deux ou de plusieurs événements contingents, chacun

This coincidental conception of chance goes probably back over Saint Thomas Aquinas, who—in his *Commentary* on Aristotle's *Metaphysics*—says that if we treat chance beings as things produced by *per se* causes, many things can be by chance, such us the intersection between independent causal lines.

As Cournot highlights, the core of this conception consists in the independence of the intersecting causal chains:

> It is necessary, to be more precise, to focus exclusively on what is fundamental and categorical in the notion of chance, namely, the idea of independence or non-solidarity among various series of causes [...].[7]

To clarify this point, let us represent the already quoted Monod's example.

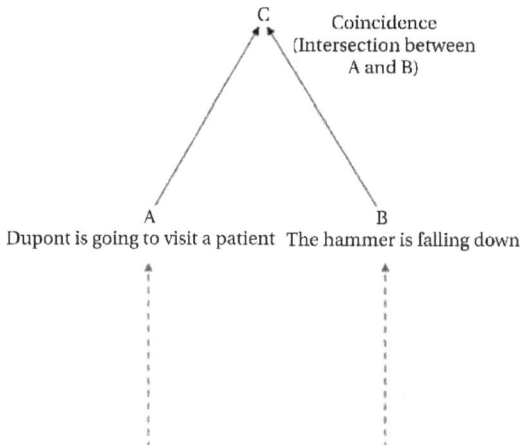

Fig. 2.1 Monod's Example of a Coincidence

In Figure 2.1,[8] Dr. Dupont is going to visit a patient for the first time. In the meanwhile, Mr. Dubois is fixing a roof in the same area. When Dr. Dupont comes across Mr. Dubois' work site, Mr. Dubois' hammer falls inadvertently down and the trajectory of the hammer intersects the trajectory of Dr. Dupont,

---

desquels a ses causes, mais en sorte que leur concours n'en a aucune que l'on connaisse. Je suis for trompé si ce n'est là ce qu'on entend lorsqu'on parle du hasard».

[7] Cournot, *Essai sur les Fondements de nos Connaissances et sur les Caractères de la Critique Philosophique*, 56. The translation is ours. The original passage in French is as follows: «Il faut, pour bien s'entendre, s'attacher exclusivement à ce qu'il y a de fondamental et de catégorique dans la notion du hasard, savoir, à l'idée de l'indépendance ou de la non-solidarité entre diverses séries de causes».

[8] Alessandra Melas, "An Ontic conception of chance in Monod's Non-Teleological Evolutionary Biological Theory", in *An Anthology of Philosophical Studies Volume 9*, ed. Patricia Hanna (Athens: Athens Institute of Education and Research, 2015), 75.

who dies. The two dotted lines in the figure represent the two independent causal histories of *A* and *B*.

To sum up, coincidences are events that can be divided into components *independently* produced by some causal factor.

It is important to remark that—although coincidences are chance events that can be *described* in causal terms—they are not nominal, because they cannot be causally *explained*. In fact, since the intersecting causal lines are independent from each other, to explain each individual causal chain is quite different from explaining the intersection between the involved chains. In Monod's example, it is possible to explain why Dr. Dupont is going to visit his patient and why Mr. Dubois' hammer is falling down, but—since the causal lines involved have independent causal histories—it is not possible to explain in causal terms the intersection between Dr. Dupont's trajectory and the hammer's trajectory. Explaining the behaviour of every single intersecting causal process is not sufficient to understand why the accident, i.e., the intersection, happened.

Let us also consider Cournot's example. A Parisian decides to go for an outing and takes a train to reach the desired location. The train goes off the rail and the Parisian is the poor victim. In this case we have an intersection between two independent causal lines: the Parisian in the train and the train which goes off the rail.

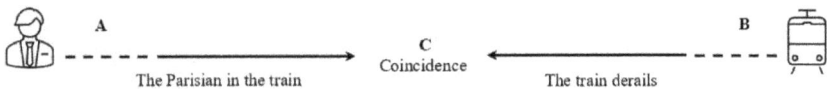

A — — — — — —————————→ C ←————— — — — — B
           The Parisian in the train   Coincidence   The train derails

Fig. 2.2 Cournot's Example of Hasard

In Figure 2.2, the intersection between *A* and *B* represents a coincidence, a coincidence which has—as its proper consequence—the Parisian's death. The dotted parts of the arrows in the figure represent the two independent causal histories of *A* and *B*.

An Ontic Conception of Chance?

As Julienne Junkersfeld maintains in his book, "if one consults standard dictionaries for the definition of the word 'chance', he finds that, according to good usage, it may have many different meanings".[9]

---

[9] M. Julienne Junkersfeld, *The Aristotelian–Thomistic concept of chance* (Notre Dame: University of Notre Dame, 1945), 1.

Sometimes, for example, the expression 'happening by chance' refers to phenomena which are fortuitous in a fundamental way, sometimes it refers to phenomena which are epistemically fortuitous.

The following Henri Poincaré's passage may be useful to clarify the distinction between a fundamental notion of chance and an epistemic one:

> And so, if the word chance is simply a synonym for ignorance, what does it mean? [...] It is therefore necessary that chance be something other than the name we give to our ignorance, that among the phenomena of which we are ignorant of the causes, we must distinguish between fortuitous phenomena, [...], and those which are not fortuitous and about which we can say nothing, as long as we have not determined the laws which govern them.[10]

What precisely is fundamental chance according to Poincaré? Fundamental (i.e., objective) chance is something which goes beyond our ignorance and, at the same time, comes from some actual feature of reality. Conversely, in the case of epistemic chance, something seems to happen by chance only because one does not have a complete knowledge about what is observed.

What about Cournot and Monod's notion of *hasard*?

According to Cournot, chance must be objective to guarantee the objectivity of probability:

> Affirming the objective reality of chance is, for Cournot, showing that probability can be applied to reality to measure not our degree of belief in the possible occurrence of an event, but the actual possibility of this event.[11]

However, at the very beginning one could think that in Cournot the discussion moves from an ontic level to an epistemic one.

---

[10] Poincaré, *Calcul des Probabilités*, 3. The translation is ours. The original passage in French is as follows: «Et alors si le mot hasard est tout simplement un synonyme d'ignorance, qu'est- ce que cela veut dire? [...] Il faut donc bien que le hasard soit autre chose que le nom que nous donnons a` notre ignorance, que parmi les phénomènes dont nous ignorons les causes, nous devions distinguer les phénomènes fortuits, [...], et ceux qui ne sont pas fortuits et sur lesquels nous ne pouvons rien dire, tant que nous n'aurons pas déterminé les lois qui les régissent».

[11] Thierry Martin, *Probabilités et Critique Philosophique selon Cournot* (Paris: Vrin, 1996), 107. The translation is ours. The original passage in French is as follows: «Affirmer la réalité objective du hasard, c'est pour Cournot, montrer que la probabilité peut s'appliquer au réel pour mesurer non pas notre degré de croyance an la réalisation possible d'un événement, mais la possibilité effective de cet événement».

In fact, as it is well quoted by Martin:

> Cournot makes it clear "the word *chance* does not indicate a substantial cause, but an idea".[12]

And:

> Strictly speaking, for Cournot, an event is never the product of chance, nor produced by chance.[13]

What does it mean? Is it not chance something that comes from some actual feature of reality?

According to Cournot's view, chance is not something like a new force, or physical object. This is exactly what Cournot wants to say when he states that the word '*hasard*' does not indicate a substance, but it indicates an idea. More precisely, as it has already shown, chance is not—following Cournot—a single thing, but it describes a situation, and it can be defined as what comes from the intersection between independent chains.

Clarified that, now we face a new problem, that is to see whether the intersecting chains are physical things or not.

According to Cournot's view, the word 'cause' is used:

> To designate everything that influences the production of an event, and no longer just to designate the causes themselves, or the efficient and truly active causes.[14]

More precisely, Cournot includes inside the (*lato sensu*) notion of causation all of the conditions and circumstances that make the action of the cause possible. But what are these conditions and circumstances? They are said to be

---

[12] Martin, *Probabilités et Critique Philosophique selon Cournot* (Paris: Vrin, 1996), 113. The translation is ours. The original passage in French is as follows: «Cournot le précise clairement "le mot de *hasard* n'indique pas une cause substantielle, mais une idée"».

[13] *Ibid.* The translation is ours. The original passage in French is as follows: «En toute rigueur, pour Cournot, un événement n'est jamais le produit du hasard, ni produit par hasard».

[14] Cournot, *Essai sur les Fondements de nos Connaissances et sur les Caractères de la Critique Philosophique*, 37. The translation is ours. The original passage in French is as follows: «Pour désigner tout ce qui influe sur la production d'un événement, et non plus seulement pour désigner les causes proprement dites, ou les causes efficientes et vraiment actives».

the reason for the action of the cause. In his *Essai*, in a discussion concerning the Principle of Causality, Cournot says:

> Just as everything must have its reason, so everything we call an event must have a cause.[15]

Hence, the Principle of Causality seems to be only a particular application of the Principle of Reason.

Cournot's distinction between cause (*stricto sensu*) and reason can be summed up in this way: a cause is—in some sense—a physically powerful thing, that is something which has the physical power to produce something else; differently, a reason is something which has an explicative function.

At first sight, cause (*stricto sensu*) and reason appear to be two different things: the former seems to be a physical thing, the latter does not. So that causation (*lato sensu*) looks like a non-totally physical and ontic thing.

However, it is very interesting to point out the fact that Cournot gives a physical meaning to the notion of reason as well. Following what Martin already said, Cournot's distinction between reasons and causes is the same as the distinction between regular causes and accidental causes:

> If we consider a fortuitous and repeatable event, like the one to which the game of heads or tails gives rise, we must distinguish, says Cournot, regular or permanent causes, which remain identical for all the tests (the regularity or the irregularity of structure part) and fortuitous or accidental causes, which vary with each test (the direction and intensity of the impulsive force).[16]

Each event is brought about by the combination of regular causes and accidental causes, which are both physical/ontic causes.

---

[15] Cournot, *Essai sur les Fondements de nos Connaissances et sur les Caractères de la Critique Philosophique*, 33. The translation is ours. The original passage in French is as follows: «De même que toute chose doit avoir sa raison, ainsi tout ce que nous appelons événement doit avoir une cause».

[16] Martin, *Probabilités et Critique Philosophique selon Cournot*, 124. The translation is ours. The original passage in French is as follows: «Si on considère un événement fortuit et répétable, comme celui auquel donne lieu le jeu de pile ou face, on doit distinguer, dit Cournot, des causes régulières ou permanentes, qui demeurent identiques pour toutes les épreuves (la régularité ou l'irrégularité de structure de la pièce) et des causes fortuites ou accidentelles, qui varient avec chaque épreuve (la direction et l'intensité de la force impulsive)».

Now go back to the definition of *hasard*, that one finds in the *Exposition*:

> The events brought about by the combination or the meeting of phenomena which belong to independent series, in the order of causality, are what are called fortuitous events, or the results of chance.[17]

In the *Essai*, there seems to be a change in that definition, a change that is proposed in the *Traité* in the following way:

> The idea of chance is the idea of an encounter between facts that are rationally independent of each other [...].[18]

There is a passage from a causal independence to a rational independence. Then, given that, are the intersecting chains still real processes? The answer to this question is positive. As we already said, Cournot gives a physical meaning even to the notion of reason. More precisely, Cournot's distinction between reasons and causes is the same as the distinction between regular causes and accidental causes, which are both physical processes.

Hence, it can be concluded that chance—according to Cournot—comes from some ontic feature of reality, in a way that chance can be an objective thing.

As we have already seen, Monod talks about "absolute coincidences", in which the use of the word 'absolute' is not fortuitous. More precisely, such a word means that there are coincidental events which would still be coincidental even though we had something like a God's-eye view, that is independently from our degree of knowledge.

To enforce the idea according to which Monod's notion of absolute coincidences is a fundamental conception, let us consider the following passage, in which the distinguished biologist puts on light a non-fundamental notion of chance in contrast with his coincidental one:

> Dice and roulette are called games of chance, and the theory of probability is used to forecast their outcome. But chance enters into

---

[17] Antoine Augustine Cournot, *Exposition de la Théorie des Chances et des Probabilités* (Paris: Hachette, 1843), 55. The translation is ours. The original passage in French is as follows: «Les événements amenés par la combinaison ou la rencontre de phénomènes qui appartiennent à des séries indépendantes, dans l'ordre de la causalité, sont ce qu'on nomme des événements fortuits, ou des résultats du hasard».

[18] Antoine Augustine Cournot, *Traité de l'Enchaînement des Idées Fondamentales dans les Sciences et dans l'Histoire* (Paris: Hachette, 1861), 62. The translation is ours. The original passage in French is as follows: «L'idée de hasard est l'idée d'une rencontre entre des faits rationnellement indépendants les uns des autres [...]».

these purely mechanical and macroscopic games only because of the practical impossibility of governing the throw of the dice or the spinning of the little ball with sufficient precision. A highly precise mechanical thrower might conceivably be invented which would go far to reduce the uncertainty of the outcome. Let us say that in roulette the uncertainty is purely *operational* and not *essential.* [...].[19]

Here the word 'essential' stays for 'fundamental' and the word 'operational' stays for 'methodological'. It seems that Monod, when he talks about "absolute coincidences", assumes an essential idea of chance and no longer merely an operational one.[20]

This view about chance and coincidences, from this perspective, can be understood as an objective one, where causal intersections are not only

---

[19] Monod, *Chance and Necessity: Essay on the Natural Philosophy of Modern Biology*, 114. The italics are ours. The original passage in French is as follows: «Le contenu de la notion de hasard n'est pas simple et le mot même est employé dans des situations très différentes. Le mieux est d'en prendre quelques exemples. Ainsi on emploie ce mot à propos du jeu de dés, ou de la roulette, et on utilise le calcul des probabilités pour prévoir l'issue d'une partie. Mais ces jeux purement mécaniques, et macroscopiques, ne sont «de hasard» qu'en raison de l'impossibilité pratique de gouverner avec une précision suffisante le jet du dé ou celui de la boule. Il est évident qu'une mécanique de lancement de très haute précision est concevable, qui permettrait d'éliminer en grande partie d'incertitude du résultat. Disons qu'à la roulette, l'incertitude est purement opérationnelle, mais non essentielle. Il en est de même, comme on le verra aisément, pour la théorie de nombreux phénomènes où on emploie la notion de hasard et le calcul des probabilités pour des raisons purement méthodologiques. Mais dans d'autres situations, la notion de hasard prend une signification essentielle et non plus simplement opérationnelle. C'est le cas, par exemple, de ce que l'on peut appeler les "coïncidences absolues" [...]» [1970].

[20] Objective chance is sometimes related in literature with the notion of objective probability, since it is a very common idea that an event which happens by chance has a very low objective probability to happen. Here the meaning of objective probability plays a very important role, and our discussion is complicated by the fact that there is a very long tradition in philosophy of science concerning the interpretation of probability and the distinction between subjective probability and objective one. Broadly speaking, there are arguably two main concepts of probability: a) the probability intended as a measure of the real, physical, tendency of something to occur; b) the probability intended as the measure of how strongly one believes something will occur. As the reader can see in Chapter 4, our best understanding of notions such as expectations is cashed out in terms of subjective probable outcomes of actions and events, and hence it is a matter of subjective probability. By the way, for a more detailed discussion on interpretations of probability the reader can refer to Alan Hájek, "The Interpretations of Probability", *The Stanford Encyclopedia of Philosophy*, 2019, https://plato.stanford.edu/entries/probability-interpret/#MaiIn

facts/events, but also play a major role in the understanding of coincidences. Since causal intersections are so important in the overall definition of this traditional approach to coincidences, it would be useful to call this tradition "intersectionism".

Chapter 3

The Very Idea of a Common Cause: From Reichenbach to Lando's Account

An Alternative to Mainstream Intersectionism

This chapter is a bit more technical and involves a detailed discussion of a conception that is especially incompatible with our view of coincidences. This incompatibility, according to us, as it entails the possibility of undermining our general account, needs detailed discussions and some principled answers. We apologise to readers who are not interested in this type of more technical and detailed discussion. Readers who are not interested in this discussion can go directly to Chapter 4 and find our main proposal.

An important challenge to the traditional view about coincidences, which understands them as intersections of independent causal lines, is based on the general "Common Cause Principle", introduced for the first time by Hans Reichenbach in 1956 in his *The Direction of Time*. Let's see what Reichenbach wrote about cases in which the simultaneous occurrence of apparently unrelated events is observed:

> The schema of this reasoning illustrates the rule that the improbable should be explained in terms of causes, [...] the logical schema that governs it may be called the *principle of the common cause*. It can be stated in the form: *If an improbable coincidence has occurred, there must exist a common cause.*[1]

Reichenbach here postulates the existence of common causes for those incidences that cannot apparently be explained by the existence of a direct causal link between the events in question. In short, the Principle of Common Cause supports the existence of common causes whenever improbable coincidences occur, and it suggests that cases in which two events occur jointly, though they are expected to be independent, must be explained by identifying the common cause responsible for the occurrence of both events in question.

---

[1] Hans Reichenbach, *The Direction of Time* (Dover: University of California Press, 1956), 157.

Along the way traced by Reichenbach, Tamar Lando's recent work provided new fuel to this conception.[2] Following the Reichenbachian view, Lando rejects and criticizes the traditional account of coincidences—meaning their constitution in terms of intersecting independent causal lines—claiming that coincidences can be explained as outcomes of what she understands as common causes. To put it differently, we can have examples of coincidences in which we do not testify to any clear intersection of independent causal lines, as these examples show coincidences as determined only by a common cause.

Moreover, but not less importantly, Lando makes a strategic move, mainly methodological, in order to avoid what she recognizes as the psychological component of a coincidence, that is, that aspect concerning coincidences as being unlikely, significant and so forth. Even though she recognises that there is something taking place in coincidences at the psychological level, she says that an investigation into this aspect will make this understanding of coincidences a bit cumbersome and lead the theorist astray—incidentally, this option presents Lando's proposal as orthogonal to ours also from a methodological perspective (see next chapter). Furthermore, and this is a major theoretical commitment, her interest is mainly devoted to the relevance of coincidences for our understanding of causality and causal explanations. This is not surprising since the traditional view about coincidences finds them especially interesting from a causal point of view, because they present a straightforward challenge to causal explanation as far as they are determined by causal intersections on the one hand but are ultimately not explained in causal terms on the other.

Hence, to get a perspicuous image of such a perspective, Lando's idea is first to cut out the psychological level of coincidences at the very beginning and to focus on what is going on at the causal level, but—and this is her second strategic move—without starting with the traditional understanding of coincidences as determined by the intersection of independent causal chains. The first point is understood as permitting Lando a closer look at the very causal structure of coincidental events, avoiding any theoretical contamination from what she deems spurious psychological considerations. However, this main focus on causality does not depend on the main idea in the tradition, namely the idea of a coincidence as a causal intersection among independent causal lines. This crucial difference alone accounts for the importance of Lando's proposal in the contemporary debate. We next explain the details of this proposal.

---

[2] Tamar Lando, "Coincidence and Common Cause", *Noûs* 51, no. 1 (2017): 132; doi: 10.11 11/nous.12166

Introducing the Common Cause: Lando's Example

Lando claims to provide straightforward counterexamples to the traditional view that defends the idea of an intersection between independent causal chains. Such counterexamples are shaped to provide direct evidence in support of the availability and tenability of coincidences determined by a common cause. If these non-intersectionist coincidences are convincing, then the popular idea that traditional intersectionism is the way to go would be undermined. Hence, a close inspection is justified. It can be difficult and too abstract to talk about such examples before introducing and discussing them, so let us proceed to the main point.

Lando presents her original example, called *Pianos*, as follows:

> ***Pianos***. A boy is playing with a ball in the courtyard of an apartment complex. He throws the ball too high, and it bounces off of the balcony of one apartment, sails through the air, bounces onto the balcony of another apartment, and finally falls to the ground. On each of the two balconies sits a grand piano. As the ball lands on the first balcony it strikes a note on the first piano, and as the ball lands on the second balcony, it strikes a note on the second piano. On each of the two pianos, the note struck is the hi A.[3]

There is an undeniably interesting coincidence taking place in this example, as the ball's two bounces, remarkably, end up hitting the same key and playing the same note on each piano. Lando interprets this example as a clear, genuine coincidence—i.e., the ball ending up playing the same note on both pianos—determined by a single common cause—i.e., the boy throwing the ball in the air. *Prima facie*, Lando achieves directly what she wants, namely a clear illustration of a coincidence in which the coincidental nature of what is occurring is non-controversial and, in particular, one that does not depend on an intersection of independent causal chains; rather, it apparently depends on a single throw of the ball, which is presented as the official common cause generating the bounces and the whole coincidence. Clearly, if Lando's description is right, then *Pianos* surely counts as a direct counterexample to the traditional view, with the upshot that we can have coincidences that are not determined by the intersection of independent causal chains. A view like this was ruled out almost *a priori* by the traditional view, so it makes a relevant difference in the global understanding of what is a coincidence: as a matter of fact, if Lando is right, this could be the counterexample capable of proving the entire traditional view wrong. Let us drill deeper into her discussion.

---

[3] Lando, "Coincidence and Common Cause", 135.

As she puts it, "[i]t is a coincidence that the same note is struck on both pianos". However, the throw of the ball "causes the first *A*-note to be struck", and the throw of the ball "causes the second *A*-note to be struck". Hence, "*the throw is a common cause* [emphasis added] of each of the coincidence's constituent events".[4] Lando concludes from this reading of her example that the traditional view is thoroughly mistaken, since we can get coincidences without admitting the necessity of causal intersections, which is the theoretical pillar of the traditional understanding. However, we can dig into this view a bit deeper. In fact, Lando also clarifies what she means exactly by the very concept of a common cause, which is of particular relevance in evaluating the goodness of the proposal: "*c* is a common cause of *e* and *f* if *c* is both a cause of *e* and a cause of *f*".[5] This means that, according to Lando, an event E playing some causal role in determining two or more events EV_1, EV_2, ... EV_n is sufficient to identify E as their common cause. Lando applies exactly this idea of a common cause in describing the example: here "[t]here is a causal path from the throw of the ball, through the striking of the first *A*-note, to the striking of the second".[6] This conception of a common cause is based directly on the idea of causal sufficiency. She reads the example as a case of an event, i.e., the throwing of the ball, which is causally sufficient to determine two other events, i.e., the bounces of the ball that end up in the *A*-note being struck twice on two different pianos—one time each.

However, this reading is not, according to us, as conclusive as Lando claims. At least *prima facie*, we think this reading is not as straightforward and self-evident as Lando takes it to be. We think, in fact, that this discussion overlooks the (causal) role of the locations of the pianos in the example. If the locations of the pianos play some causal role, then, after all, there is some causal intersection going on, and intersectionism would be reinstated. Therefore, at the end of the day, do the positions of the pianos play some salient causal role in *Pianos*?

Lando starts discussing her example by stating that the locations of the pianos are not causally salient:[7] this option is dismissed at the very beginning before addressing the main alternatives that she sees as more relevant in contrasting her view about the common cause. Even before dismissing the causal relevance of the positions of the pianos, Lando already makes a general point that is indicative of her attitude about causal salience: "Here we distinguish

---

[4] *Ibid.*
[5] *Ibid.*
[6] *Ibid.*
[7] *Ibid.*

salient causes—sometimes referred to as *the* cause of an event—from other "causal factors" or mere background conditions".[8] This is indeed a sound distinction of the utmost relevance when investigating causal matters. Nonetheless, it exposes genuine difficulties: How can we reliably draw a distinction between salient causes and background conditions? One always needs to rely on compelling criteria to do this. Lando includes an example from Hart and Honoré about oxygen being a background condition for the start of a fire.[9] Well, certainly, this is an excellent example that picks up a non-controversial background condition. It is very interesting that she could not exploit *Pianos* to make a point like this. This is the first alarm bell. We think she is obliged to change the example because in *Pianos*, the distinction between what is salient and what is not is somewhat blurry, and the criteria for the distinction are not that explicit. An interesting consequence of her attitude is that the positions of the pianos in *Pianos* are taken as nothing more than a background condition, while the throw of the ball is understood as the only cause of the coincidence. However, later in the discussion, Lando endorses a counterfactual view about causation in order to defend the causal salience of the throw of the ball. We agree wholeheartedly with this. However, if the counterfactual reading is correct, this view about the common cause is untenable, and her example is not compelling as a requirement to reach the correct causal reading of *Pianos*. In fact, the counterfactual view defends the positions of the pianos as being causally salient as well (see below). However, let us explore further the details of her discussion, in which Lando offers additional reasons to deny any causal salience to the positions of the pianos.

She dismisses the causal salience of the positions of the pianos by providing two further counterexamples. The first example deals with the possibility that the pianos 1) have been in their positions for a wider amount of time, e.g., something like 75 years; and 2) that they weigh several tons each, so that no one could have easily moved them here and there. She states that in this modified version of *Pianos*, the throw of the ball is unequivocally the salient common cause, while the positions of the pianos seem to be clearly a background condition.

Two main remarks need to be made soon. First, by this very modification, Lando implicitly admits that in *Pianos* it is not natural at all to understand the positions of the pianos as a background condition: that is, they intuitively play a causal role, as we feel compelled to judge. Second, we do not find the argument convincing, even in the modified scenario: the fact that the pianos

---

[8] Lando, "Coincidence and Common Cause", 134.

[9] *Ibid.*

cannot be moved is nowhere near the level of evidence we need to see that they do not play any causal role in *Pianos*.

Imagine something along the lines of Hume's famous examples of billiard balls:[10] we have a ball *C*, which is the one that we hit, then there are two further balls, *D* on the right and *E* on the left. *C* hits *D* first and then bounces on *E*, hitting it, and both *D* and *E* fall down the same hole. Imagine a modified version in which *D* and *E* are glued to the pool table: in this case, the very same causal trajectory that in the former example ended up pushing both *D* and *E* down the same hole does not yield the same result. What is the role of causation in these examples? *D* and *E* play a causal role both in the original and the modified versions of the example: in the first example, the position of *D* is causally relevant in determining the bounce that ends up with it first hitting *E* and then rolling down the hole; and the position of *E* is causally relevant in determining the trajectory of *E* down the hole. In the modified version of the example, the fact that *D* and *E* are glued to the pool table determines a different causal system and a different causal outcome, but this does not mean that *D* and *E* are not causally relevant when glued to the pool table. They causally determine another result, one in which *C* bounces in a different way and does not determine any further bounces in *D* and *E*. These are causal intersections—period. The glue itself plays a causal role. The same goes for the modified version of *Pianos* in which the pianos cannot be moved. The fact that they cannot be moved does not avoid their positions as causally salient (see below for a defence of this view based on a counterfactual approach). Therefore, according to our intuitions, this example does not work in dismissing the locations of the pianos from being causally salient. Hence, the locations of the pianos are causally salient.

In the second example, Lando posits that there is an explicit common cause determining the positions of the pianos so that these are not supposed to be causally independent of one another. Her example concerns heavy keyboards, instead of pianos, that are dropped by the pilot of a plane low on fuel who desperately needs to reduce the cargo. These keyboards fall down to the balconies occupying the same positions as the pianos in *Pianos*. According to this version, "the pilot's shove is the common cause of the first and second keyboards being positioned in the way they are".[11] Despite this further common cause, striking the same note on both keyboards still counts as a coincidence. Hence, she argues, the way in which the keyboards landed on the

---

[10] David Hume, *An Inquiry Concerning Human Understanding* (New York: The Bobbs-Merrill Co., 1955[1740]), 40, 44, 187-188.

[11] Lando, "Coincidence and Common Cause", 136.

balconies does not make the event less coincidental than in the original version of *Pianos.* She concludes that in this scenario, "none of the salient causes of one of the constituent events" is independent of the "salient causes of the other constituent event".[12]

Here, we can surely notice that with this new modification, the causal system changes significantly from *Pianos.* Now we have the throw of the ball on the one hand and the pilot dropping the keyboards to their locations on the other. These causal chains intersect because of the trajectories of the throw and the positions where the keyboards land, determining the coincidence. Even though there is a common cause for the determination of the positions of the keyboards, this becomes a causal line that is independent of the throw of the ball and intersects it by positioning the keyboards in that way. Thus, we have two clear causal lines: a) the throw of the ball (with its specific trajectory); and b) the landing of the keyboards (in their specific positions). Sure enough, such lines are mutually independent. Finally, such independent lines intersect when the ball strikes the first *A*-note and determines a bounce that ends up striking the second *A*-note. Hence, our reading delivers two interesting results: 1) this seems a straightforward vindication of the traditional view; and, especially, 2) the example goes nowhere near dismissing the causal salience of the positions of the keyboards/pianos. The fact that the keyboards landed in those positions in the way they did does not affect the role they play in the coincidence and does nothing to show that the locations are not causally salient: they remain salient for a very intuitive and strong reason, namely that had these locations been different, we would not notice any coincidence (more on this below). Hence, the locations of the pianos are causally salient.

Therefore, Lando's dismissal of the causal role of the locations of the pianos that leads her to declare that these are not causally salient is not only too quick but also quite mistaken. This quick dismissal plays a pivotal role in her argument by getting rid, very soon, of what we see as the main contender for defending the traditional intersectionist view and permitting her to feel free to focus on very weak contenders, which are presented as the relevant alternatives to the common cause view. These alternatives, presented as the main contenders, which she takes to be relevant, claim that "(a) it is *not* a coincidence that the same note was struck on the pianos", or that "(b) the constituents of the purported coincidence do not have a common cause".[13] Let us claim soon that (a) is very weak, and we think that no one would endorse it as both implausible and counterintuitive. So, of these two contenders, only (b) deserves some lines

---

[12] *Ibid.*
[13] *Ibid.*

of discussion, as it significantly intersects somewhat with our favourite line of argument.

We see such alternatives in general as weak and not so intuitive, while at the same time we see the assigning of a causal role also to the locations of the pianos as much more relevant here. So, as a matter of fact, we will not deal in depth with Lando's discussion of the views she identifies as the main contenders and will return mainly to the issue of the locations of the pianos. To be fair, something of what we are going to say will directly intersect the problem raised by Lando's (b) option: in fact, even though the throw of the ball is surely a salient and (temporally) first cause of what happens in *Pianos*, we affirm both that the positions of the pianos are causally salient and that these positions are not caused by the throw of the ball, and hence the throw of the ball is not the common cause of *Pianos*. However, let us proceed along a more linear trajectory. This is just a first hint of our take on the causal system involved in *Pianos*, and we will say more about this after discussing in more depth the issue about the causal salience of the positions of the pianos. So, let us dig deeper into the issue of the pianos' causal salience.

The view that defends the causal salience of the positions of the pianos, we believe, can, in principle, vindicate the traditional intersectionist position. Furthermore, the special way in which Lando vindicates the causal role of the throw of the ball as genuine, which is defended in terms of counterfactual conditionals according to Lewis' counterfactual view on causation,[14] also vindicates, according to our point of view, the causal salience of the locations of the pianos. The counterfactual view of causation, as Lando resumes Lewis's account, affirms that "an event *e* counterfactually depends on an event *c* if, had *c* not occurred, *e* would not have occurred".[15] We agree that this principle is strongly intuitive, and we basically agree on the counterfactual dependences

---

[14] David Lewis, *Philosophical Papers. Vol. II* (Oxford: Oxford University Press, 1987). We do not endorse Lewis' counterfactual account of causation, though it is usefully exploited to show how much counterfactual considerations point in the direction of admitting the causal salience of the locations of the pianos. A problem of Lewis' account surely depends on its metaphysical entailments and putative complications, e.g., his modal realism concerning the actual existence of possible worlds. We do not want to enter into these complications, and just rely more generally on quite generic counterfactual considerations about the causal salience of the locations of the pianos. Lewis' view is introduced by Lando, and we just wish to highlight that such insertion does not easily fit with the desired outcome (that is, with the defence of the common cause, see below). We thank an anonymous reviewer for pointing this problem out.

[15] Lando, "Coincidence and Common Cause", 137. See also, for the full account, Lewis, *Philosophical Papers. Vol. II*, 159-213, 214-240.

enacted by causal relations.[16] However, we have insights about the possibility of defending the genuine causal salience of the locations of the pianos based on the very same grounds. This is enough, we believe, to dig a bit deeper into the putative causal role of the locations of the pianos, which was quickly dismissed by Lando as not causally salient.[17]

Our main hypothesis, as anticipated above, is that the causal system responsible for what is going on in *Pianos* is not reduced solely to the throw of the ball as a common cause—even though we recognise that the throw of the ball plays an undeniably effective causal role in all that happens in the example. The idea that we find intuitive is that the causal system here is wider than the throw of the ball alone, also comprising the locations of the pianos as making a causal difference in what happens in *Pianos*. The bouncing of the ball in certain locations, intuitively, seems to be causally relevant, because had these locations been even slightly different, we would not have attended to a coincidence, the eventual notes struck would have been different, and so forth. The throw of the ball and the locations of the pianos here play the role of steps of causal dependence—in Lewis' phrase.[18] A particular effect—in this case, the two *A*-notes being struck on both pianos—need not depend on a cause directly, and in fact we can change the outcome of the causal event by changing the locations of the pianos. This means that we need a different reading of the relevant causal system in *Pianos*. Therefore, the general hypothesis that we endorse as the correct identification of the relevant causal system, which differs from Lando's, is as follows:

> Revised hypothesis to reshape a reading of *Pianos*:
> Salient causal system = throw of the ball + bounces of the ball on certain locations/keys.

---

[16] We are aware that there are different views on counterfactual conditionals on the table, and that they present problems and challenges. We do not want to open that controversial discussion here and just rely on an intuitive reading of counterfactuals which is useful for the discussion of Lando's examples. We, following Lewis together with people with very different ideas about counterfactuals, are just happy to take counterfactual conditionals at face value, as statements about possible alternatives concerning the relevant facts. For a different account of counterfactual conditionals, more in line with our metaphysical tastes, see Marc Lange, *Laws and Lawmakers. Science, Metaphysics, and the Laws of Nature* (Oxford: Oxford University Press, 2009).

[17] Lando, "Coincidence and Common Cause", 135-36.

[18] Lewis, *Philosophical Papers. Vol. II*, 179. Again, the fact that we find Lewis' phrase compelling here does not mean that we adhere to his view on counterfactuals, but just that counterfactual considerations are generally very useful to highlight our doubts about the common cause view (see below).

This interpretative perspective is firstly motivated by some considerations dealing with the counterfactual account of causation that Lando endorses, but we think such considerations are sound based on more general counterfactual considerations about causal transitions (hence, by our lights, these do not depend on endorsing a particular view). In fact, she directly defends the causal salience of the throw of the ball in terms of certain counterfactual conditionals that, we agree, clearly certify the salience of the throw of the ball in playing a genuinely non-controversial causal role in *Pianos*. She dismisses the locations of the pianos as causally salient before entering into the discussion of the counterfactual view of causation. However, as a matter of fact, counterfactual conditionals analogous to those that certify the causal salience of the throw of the ball also certify, very generally, the causal salience of the locations of the pianos. Let us present Lando's examples correctly used to defend the throw's causal salience.

Lando exploits the following counterfactual conditionals:

(A) Had the ball not been thrown, note *A* on Piano 1 would not have been struck.

(B) Had the ball not been thrown, note *A* on Piano 2 would not have been struck.[19]

This is indeed an elegant and efficacious way to make the throw's causal role fully explicit and vindicate its genuine causal salience in what is going on in *Pianos*. We could not agree more with Lando here, and we think this is an excellent way to make the point about the causal salience of the throw of the ball. So far, so good. However, this, we think, has entailments that go well beyond Lando's perspective and that may ultimately undermine her idea of a common cause as a correct description of the causal system in *Pianos*. In fact, by these very criteria, the partial causal role played by the positions of the pianos supports the very same type of counterfactual conditionals:

(C) Had the first piano been located 10 cm to the left, note *A* on Piano 1 would not have been struck.

(D) Had the second piano been located 10 cm to the left, note *A* on Piano 2 would not have been struck.[20]

---

[19] Lando, "Coincidence and Common Cause", 136.

[20] As Lewis would comment on this "[...] if the cause had not been, the effect never had existed" (Lewis, *Philosophical Papers. Vol. II*, 159). Lewis reads this counterfactual conditional as expressing the general relation of causal dependence (*Ivi*, 167). We think that this statement can be made without the need to endorse Lewis' account.

If *A* and *B* are taken to imply that the throwing of the ball plays an undeniably genuine and salient causal role, then *C* and *D* also show, by the very same mechanism and internal logic, that the positions of the pianos play a genuine and salient causal role. Therefore, the problem is as follows: Why does Lando think that the positions of the pianos are not causally salient when these conform unproblematically to the counterfactual view that she embraces for the causal salience of the throw of the ball? We think that this depends on Lando's quick dismissal of the locations before her introduction and discussion of the counterfactual view that she rightly exploits to certify the causal salience of the throw of the ball. However, as stated, the very fact that we can perform a straightforward analysis of the locations' causal role in counterfactual terms is evidence that Lando's dismissal of the locations' causal salience has been too quick and ultimately turns out to be misleading.

The fact that the locations of the pianos are causally salient can also be vindicated from different points of view, which provide independent grounds to defend the counterfactual view of causation. For example, denying the salience of the locations of the pianos turns out to be misleading, especially if we analyse causation by appealing to the notion of manipulation.[21] A common-sense idea about causation is that causal relationships are potentially exploitable for purposes of manipulation and control: very roughly, if *C* is genuinely a cause of *E*, then if I can manipulate *C* in the right way, this should be a way of manipulating or changing *E*.[22] First, interventionist versions of manipulability

---

[21] We are not going to raise more general issues about the troublesome connections between causal salience and background conditions. As philosophers of science know, the issue is especially controversial and complicated. In this context, we limit ourselves to non-controversial cases, but we are aware of possible complications: we leave such complications open for other occasions. Those readers interested in this particular issue can see, for example, Paul Noordhof, "Probabilistic Causation, Preemption, and Counterfactuals", *Mind* 108, no. 429 (1999): 95; Peter Menzies, "Causation in Context", in *Causation, Physics, and the Constitution of Reality*, ed. Huw Price and Richard Corry (Oxford: Oxford University Press, 2007), 191-223. We thank an anonymous reviewer for pointing this out.

[22] See for example Robin George Collingwood, *An Essay in Metaphysics* (Oxford: Oxford University Press, 1940); Douglas Gasking, "Causation and Recipes", *Mind* 64, no. 256 (1955), 479; Peter Menzies and Huw Price, "Causation as a Secondary Quality", *British Journal for the Philosophy of Science* 44, no. 2 (1993): 187; George von Wright, *Causality and Determinism* (New York: Columbia University Press, 1975); Judea Pearl, *Causality* (New York: Cambridge University Press, 2000); James Woodward, *Making Things Happen: A Theory of Causal Explanation* (Oxford: Oxford University Press, 2003); James Woodward, "Causation and Manipulability", *The Stanford Encyclopedia of Philosophy*, 2016, https://plato.stanford.edu/entries/causation-mani/. For a recent overview see also Huw Price, "Causation, Intervention, and Agency: Woodward on Menzies and Price", in *Making a*

theories are counterfactual theories. The characterisation of an intervention tells us what should be envisioned as changed and what should be held fixed when we evaluate the sorts of counterfactuals that are relevant to elucidating causal claims, such as: "If X were to be changed by an intervention to such and such a value, the value of Y would change". Second, and most importantly, in some versions of manipulability theory, the notion of an intervention should be understood without reference to human action, and this permits the formulation of a manipulability theory that applies to causal claims in situations in which manipulation by human beings is not a practical possibility.

Those simple insights turn the tables on Lando's account and readmit, according to us, the actual main contender against her view. That is, our reading of *Pianos* rehabilitates the traditional conception, which here is the basic idea that the positions of the pianos play some genuine causal role in determining the coincidence. From this premise, we can go straight back to intersectionism, but let us first explore the entailments for the common cause.

Intersectionism Vindicated

If we are right that the locations of the pianos play a genuine and salient causal role in what is going on in *Pianos*, then we have reason to take a step back from Lando's view about assigning to the throw of the ball the role of a (genuine) common cause for what goes on in *Pianos*. This could become a straightforward reason to reject the very idea of a common cause. In fact, it would certify that *Pianos* is not evidence of a coincidence described in terms of a common cause, and so that there are no relevant counterexamples to the traditional intersectionist view. Hence, the upshot of the discussion turns out to be a general vindication of intersectionism.

Let us re-examine *Pianos* in view of this new perspective: we now have a causal system that is composed certainly by the throw of the ball as the causal event that is the starting point of what is going to happen in *Pianos*, but that does not alone determine the coincidental outcome. The specific locations of the pianos also play a causal role in determining the coincidental event. The bounces of the ball, in fact, in order to be causally responsible for the coincidental outcome, also depend on the exact locations of the pianos—and the outcome would have been different had those pianos been located somewhere else. This means that, again, and in general agreement with the traditional intersectionist view, we have different causal lines that intersect: 1) the throw

Difference: Essays on the Philosophy of Causation, ed. Helen Beebee, Christopher Hitchcock, and Huw Price (Oxford: Oxford University Press, 2017), https://doi.org/10.1093/oso/978 0198746911.003.0005.

of the ball; 2) the ball hitting the location of the first piano (playing the *A*-note) and bouncing down; and 3) the ball hitting the location of the second piano (playing the *A*-note) and bouncing down again. This is so because you can alter *Pianos* by eliminating any of these causal components (1–3) and systematically fail to get the coincidence, so we take this as manifest evidence that it does not depend only on the throw of the ball. We need a wider causal system, we need more causal lines, and, therefore, we need an intersectionist account that is more in line with the traditional view.

Furthermore, if we analyse the causal components (1–3), we realise that they are, in an important sense, mutually independent from a causal point of view. In fact, the single locations of the pianos are independent of the trajectory of the throw of the ball until there are the relevant collisions. Thus, perfectly in line with the traditional view, we get both the independence of the causal lines and their causal intersection. Coincidences are still determined by the intersection of independent causal chains. More precisely, here the coincidence is represented by the fact that we have a causal incidence of some things: in this specific case, an incidence between the ball hitting the first piano (playing the *A*-note) and bouncing down and the ball hitting the location of the second piano (playing the *A*-note) and bouncing down again, at almost the same time, but in different spaces (the two different pianos). Let's call this "time-coincidence", or maybe we already have a name for it, which is *synchronicity*!

This kind of situation drives us to think that, sometimes, what is important is neither the match in space nor the match in time (or the match in space and time); rather, what seems very important is the relation in meaning among events/facts. There must be an incidence between some things that have the same or similar meaning or content, such as the exact same *A*-note struck two times in a quick interval of time. Striking particular notes here is "significant" for us. This also means that reinstating the traditional intersectionist view can be the starting point for reconsidering another aspect that is somewhat jeopardised by Lando's account, that is, the psychological considerations surrounding coincidences. However, the meaning and significance of coincidences will be investigated in more depth in the next chapter.

Chapter 4

Hart, Honoré, and the Hybrid Alternatives

Beyond Intersectionism

At this point of our investigation, we acknowledged a main philosophical tradition that we called 'intersectionism', in which coincidences are understood mainly in terms of intersections between independent causal lines. We also saw that this dominant theoretical paradigm has been challenged by a different view, according to which we have examples of coincidences which are determined by common causes, and the defenders of this approach see this fact as direct evidence of the untenability of intersectionism. However, we claimed that such counterexamples can be adequately treated and understood within an interactionist framework, thus liberating intersectionism from this burden. Does this mean that intersectionism remains the unchallenged paradigmatic understanding of coincidences? We think that this would be too quick a conclusion and that there are, at this point, still many questions on the table regarding intersectionism—questions that, in principle, can lead us to doubt strict intersectionism and to reconsider certain intuitions provided by Hart and Honoré.

The main questions we explore in this chapter are the following:

1. The ontic dimension of coincidences:

    Are there intersections between truly independent causal sequences? Even if we state that there are some intersections between independent causal lines, one may say that the independence is not real, but only illusory. Thus, this question deals with the nature of the independence between the involved causal transitions. We will see whether the physical causal chains can really be independent or whether they depend, for example, upon a range of common causes.[1]

2. The epistemic dimension of coincidences:

    a. How important is the role of epistemic access in identifying the independence between causal lines?

        If we admit that ontic coincidences do not exist, since coincidences are "objects" constituted by an ontic part—that is, the intersection between independent physical causal lines—plus epistemic parts,

---

[1] We will explore this possibility independently of Lando's discussion on the same issue.

in a world without minds and without subjects having any epistemic access, it does not make any sense to talk about coincidences.

b. How important is the degree of epistemic access in identifying the independence of causal lines?

Concerning this question, the following must be said: there could be intersections between independent causal lines, but as our knowledge is insufficient, we tend to consider them to be intersections between non-independent causal lines. Conversely, there could be intersections between non-independent causal lines, but as our knowledge is insufficient, we tend to consider them to be intersections between independent causal lines. This means, for example, that for an agent A, an event comes from the intersection between independent causal chains (and maybe A is right in believing this), while for an agent B, the same event comes from the intersection between non-independent causal chains (and maybe B is wrong about the nature of this non-independence).

3. The collateral aspects of the epistemic dimension of coincidences:

Is there something more in coincidences than intersections between independent causal lines and epistemic access? Are concepts such as relevance, beliefs, and so on, necessary in order to consider an event a coincidence?

The epistemic and doxastic background is quite important in choosing the causal lines involved. The way we perceive and conceptualize things has a strong impact on our selection among causal lines. As a matter of fact, every intersection can be a coincidence, such as the fact that my house is next to the bakery and the fact that my school is next to the post office. Why is a hammer dropping from the roof and beating the pavement of the street not usually considered as being a coincidence, whereas Mr. Dubois' hammer falling down and hitting Dr. Dupont's head is conceived as a coincidence? Maybe because the latter is much more impressive and shocking for us than the former? Our perceptions and feelings play a crucial role in handling such situations. Thus, mere intersections among independent causal lines are not sufficient to fully determine whether an event is a coincidence. There is something more in coincidences—something at the mental level—that makes an event a coincidence.

This book aims to show the following: (a) the independence of involved physical causal lines is a constitutive part of coincidences; and (b) epistemic aspects, such as epistemic access, expectations, relevance, and so on, are also constitutive elements of coincidences (Fig. 4.1).

To make things clearer, consider the following:

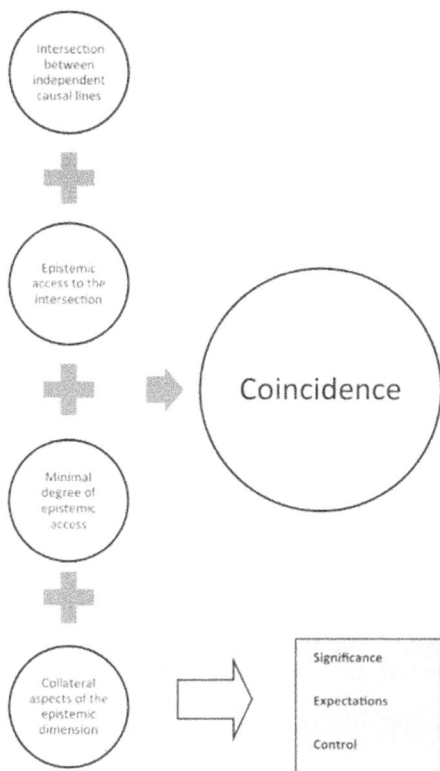

Fig. 4.1 The Constitutive Elements of Coincidences

Thus, on the one hand, we face that physical causal intersections are the basis of what we call the ontic dimension of coincidences. On the other hand, we face the need for a mind to acknowledge that an intersection is a coincidence, and this is the basis of the epistemic dimension of coincidences. As we will see, both these dimensions pose a series of conditions.

The Ontic Dimension: Are There Intersections Between Truly Independent Causal Sequences? Some Degrees of Causal Independence

One of the big problems in philosophy, as well as for our understanding of reality, is the nature of causality. There are many conceptions of causality, and no account is considered as dominant in the debate. This book will not engage in a philosophical discussion concerning that problem. Concerning causality, we endorse generally a realist point of view, according to which the order of causes is an objective feature of the world.[2] Starting from this realist point of view, the relevant problem deals with the nature and scope of the independence between the involved causal chains: Are intersections between independent causal lines really possible?

Considering Monod's example again, the intersection between Dr. Dupont's trajectory and the hammer's trajectory could be an intersection between independent causal chains. And this intersection would count as an example of the view defending the general possibility of causal independence. On the other hand, a subject could wrongly attribute independence to certain causal chains, even though these are not, in fact, independent. For example, there could be a common cause, or a range of common causes, in the past of the intersecting causal lines. This point should be analysed in more depth, in order to understand how much some common causes can affect the independence of the causal lines.

The idea of a common cause, or of a range of common causes, can be defined in different ways, composing a spectrum of options. These options show, on one side, the idea of a common cause or a range of common causes as totally affecting the independence of the causal sequences, and on the other side, the idea of a common cause or a range of common causes that, in different degrees, make independent the causal forks,[3] which go on, exponentially, getting more and more complex. More precisely, when we think of the degree of independence between the intersecting causal lines, we deal with two main options:

- The independence is global: There is no direct, or indirect, causal link between the converging causal lines we take into consideration, and the causal lines involved do not share any direct, or indirect, common cause in their past.

- The independence is local: There is some indirect, but not direct, causal link between the converging causal lines we take into consideration, or the causal lines involved share some indirect common cause in their past. In this case, the causal lines can share a common cause, but—since this common cause is ancient—it does not have any explanatory power: it can explain why the distinct causal processes are

---

[2] Since our target is to show that coincidences are at least partly mind-dependent events, and since antirealist conceptions of causality would reach this result a priori, the interesting challenge for our view is to inspect whether these results can also be reached from this realist conception. So, our commitment to realism here plays a methodological role.

[3] By forks, we mean the causal lines that at certain points intersect and then converge.

given (Dr. Dupont going to visit a patient, and the hammer falling down), but it does not explain why they match.[4]

To specify the meaning of the word 'direct', it may be useful to employ the definition of what Patrick Suppes,[5] in his outstanding contribution on the subject entitled *A Probabilistic Theory of Causality*, called 'direct causes': [...] *An event $B_{t'}$ is a direct cause of A_t if and only if $B_{t'}$ is a prima facie cause[6] of A_t and there is no t" and no partition (subset) $\pi_{t''}$ such that for every $C_{t''}$ in $\pi_{t''}$*

   i.   *$t'<t''<t$,*

   ii.   *$P(B_{t'}C_{t''})>0$,*

   iii. *$P(A_t|C_{t''}B_{t'}) = P(A_t|C_{t''})$.*[7]

That is, if and only if:

   i.   The time *t'* comes before the time *t"*, which in turn comes before time *t*,

   ii.   The probability of the conjunction of the event *B* at the time *t'* with the event *C* at time *t"* is greater than 0,

   iii. The probability of the event *A* at time *t*, given the occurrence of *C* at time *t"* and *B* at time *t'*, is equal to the probability of *A* at *t*, given the occurrence of *C* at t"; i.e., *C* screens off *A* from *B*.

More precisely, a direct causal link between, for example, *A* and *B* is a link that is not intercepted by any intermediary *I*, and a direct common cause *D* of *A* and *B* is a common cause that is not intercepted by any intermediary *A'* between *A* and *D* or by any intermediary *B'* between *B* and *D*.

---

[4] This view is supported by the distinction between causation and causal explanation, of which a quite complete and detailed illustration is provided in Lando, "Coincidence and Common Cause". See Chapter 3 for a detailed discussion.

[5] Patrick Suppes, *A Probabilistic Theory of Causality* (Amsterdam: North-Holland Publishing, 1970).

[6] According to Suppes (*A Probabilistic Theory of Causation*, 12):

The event $B_{t'}$ is a prima facie cause of the event A_t if and only if:

   (i)   the time *t'* comes before the time *t*,

   (ii) the probability of the event *B* at time *t'* is greater than 0,

   (iii) the probability of the event *A* at time *t*, given the occurrence of *B* at time *t'*, is greater than the probability of *A* at time *t*, i.e., the occurrence of *B* at *t'* improves the probability of the occurrence of *A* at *t*.

[7] Suppes, *A Probabilistic Theory of Causation*, 28.

The following Figs. 4.2, 4.3 can make that clearer:[8]

Intersection between A and B

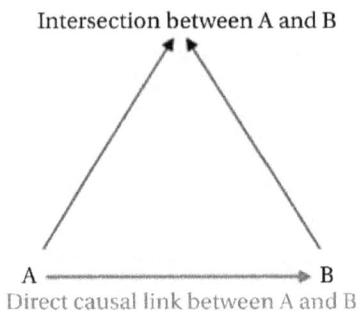

Direct causal link between A and B

Fig. 4.2 Direct Causal Link

Intersection between A and B

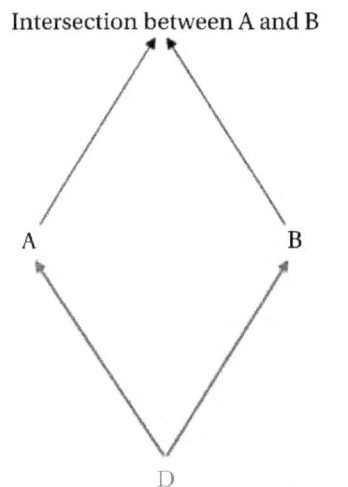

Direct common cause of A and B

Fig. 4.3 Direct Common Cause

Whereas an indirect causal link between *A* and *B* is a link that is intercepted by some intermediary *I*; and an indirect common cause *D* of *A* and *B* is a common cause that is intercepted by some intermediary *A'* between *A* and *D*, or by some intermediary *B'* between *B* and *D*.

---

[8] Melas and Salis, "On the Nature of Coincidental Events", 151. See also Chapter 2 of this book. For a different exploitation of the connection between common cause and causal intermediaries see Lando, "Coincidence and Common Cause".

The following Figs. 4.4, 4.5 can make that clearer (Melas 2017: 690):[9]

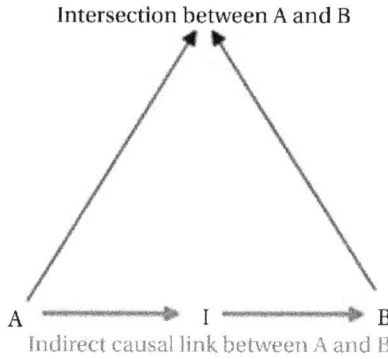

Intersection between A and B

A ⟶ I ⟶ B

Indirect causal link between A and B

Fig. 4.4 Indirect Causal Link

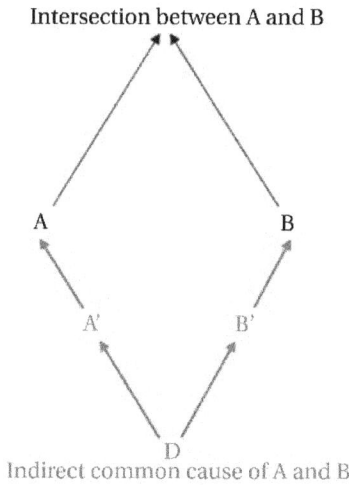

Intersection between A and B

A   B

A'   B'

D

Indirect common cause of A and B

Fig. 4.5 Indirect Common Cause

Now, we can explicate the global independence between two processes, *A* and *B*, which belong to different causal chains in the following terms. *A* and *B* are *globally* independent if they are probabilistically independent so that the following is true:

$P(A|B) = P(A)$

---

[9] Melas, "An Ontic conception of chance in Monod's Non-Teleological Evolutionary Biological Theory", 78. See also Chapter 2 of this book.

and

$P(B|A) = P(B)$.

The probabilistic independence between A and B is not due to any intermediary I of A and B. Hence, the following is not true:

$P(A|B \wedge I) = P(A|I)$

and

$P(B|A \wedge I) = P(B|I)$.

Moreover, the probabilistic independence is not due to any screening-off common cause in the past of A and B. Therefore, in this case, the probabilistic independence is not *conditional* but *absolute*.[10] As a matter of fact, given a screening-off common cause, A and B are probabilistically independent of each other.

The local independence admits the existence of ancient common causes and indirect causal links between the processes involved. So, given any intermediary I of A and B:

$P(A|B \wedge I) = P(A|I)$

and

$P(B|A \wedge I) = P(B|I)$.

Moreover, given any indirect common cause D of A and B, any intermediary A' between A and D, and any intermediary B' between B and D:

$P(A|B \wedge B' \wedge A' \wedge D) = P(A|B' \wedge A' \wedge D)^{11} = P(A|A' \wedge D)^{12} = P(A|A')$

and

$P(B|A \wedge A' \wedge B' \wedge D) = P(B|A' \wedge B' \wedge D)^{13} = P(B|B' \wedge D)^{14} = P(B|B')$.

In this case, the independence is not *absolute* but *conditional*. A and B are independent given any intermediary between A and B or any intermediary between a common cause D and A and a common cause D and B. Otherwise, the following is true:

---

[10] (Reichenbach, *The Direction of Time*, 160-61).

[11] This is because B' is an intermediary of B and D in a way that it screens off B from D.

[12] This is because D screens off A' from B'.

[13] This is because A' is an intermediary of A and D in a way that it screens off A from D.

[14] This is because D screens off B' from A'.

$$P(A|B) = P(A)$$

and

$$P(B|A) = P(B).[15]$$

This kind of independence very closely resembles a description given by Cournot:

> A man has, from his father and mother, two sets of ancestors; and in ascending order, the paternal and maternal lines branch off to each generation. He can become—in turn—the origin or the joint author of several descendant lines, which—once from the common source—will not cross over anymore, or will cross accidentally, by family alliances. In a lapse of time, each family or genealogical line contracts alliances with a multitude of other lines; but many lines, in much larger quantity, spread collaterally, remaining perfectly distinct and isolated from each other [...].[16]

This example emphasizes the potentially very complex outcome of the diverging of trajectories from a common cause or a range of common causes. The case for human generation and proliferation shows a succession of diverging causal interventions. What happens earlier can hardly be used *exclusively* to account for the complex intersections that come later.

Thus, although in many cases we are not able to admit *global* independence, we are at least able to admit local independence.

Furthermore, we can also talk about something like partial independence between the causal lines involved. Concerning that, the following quotation from Owens is very interesting:

---

[15] For a more detailed account of this approach see Melas, "Cournot's Notion of Hasard: An Objective Conception of Chance".

[16] Cournot, *Essai sur les Fondements de nos Connaissances et sur les Caractères de la Critique Philosophique*, 51. The original passage in French is as follows: «Un homme tient, par ses père et mère, a deux séries d'ascendants; et dans l'ordre ascendant, les lignes paternelle et maternelle se bifurquent a` chaque génération. Il peut devenir a` son tour la souche ou l'auteur commun de plusieurs lignes descendants qui, une fois issues de la souche commune, ne se croiseront plus, ou ne se croiseront qu'accidentellement, par des alliances de famille. Dans le laps du temps, chaque famille ou chaque faisceau généalogique contracte des alliances avec une multitude d'autre ; mais d'autre faisceaux, en bien plus grand nombre, se propagent collatéralement, en restant parfaitement distincts et isolés les uns des autres [...]».

> But there are many events [...] whose components share some, but not
> all, of their causal ancestors. Consider the fact that I am on the same
> cruise as my old enemy. [...] Perhaps a full explanation of why I am on
> that cruise will have nothing in common with a full explanation of why
> he is on that cruise. But this is unlikely. Suppose that I am cruising
> partially because the weather is hot and I wish to escape to the cool sea.
> This may well be why he is cruising also. So there is at least one causal
> factor which is relevant both to my presence and to his presence on the
> liner. [...] He is on that particular boat partly because it is calling at ports
> adjacent to antiquities which would bore me, but he has not heard of
> the liner's well-known jazz band which I am looking forward to hearing.
> So there are causal factors which are relevant to my presence but not to
> his, and vice versa.[17]

This preliminary assessment of possibilities related to causal independence
has an immediate upshot: *it is not a priori mandatory to dismiss the very idea
of an independence of causal lines*. There is room, in principle, for an effective
mutual independence between causal chains.

The Epistemic Dimension: Are Coincidences Mind-Dependent?

As already introduced, the epistemic and doxastic background is quite important
in choosing the causal lines involved in the relevant intersections we are after.
The way we perceive, understand, and conceptualize things has a strong
impact on, and many implications for, our selection among causal lines—with
different interests and (conceptual) resources, we would select different features
and lines. As a matter of fact, every intersection can be, in principle, a
coincidence, such as the fact that my house is next to the bakery, the fact that
my school is next to the post office, the fact that my bike is identical with
Alfred's, and the fact that today the TV is broadcasting the very same movie I
was thinking about this morning. *Why* is a hammer dropping from the roof and
beating the pavement of the street *not* usually considered as being a
coincidence, whereas Mr. Dubois' hammer falling down and hitting Dr.
Dupont's head is conceived instead as a coincidence? This question strikes us
as cutting the issue pretty deep. Maybe we have these insights because the
latter example is much more impressive, shocking, and bearing relevant
consequences for us than the former? Our perceptions, interests, and feelings
play a crucial role in order to handle such situations. If causal intersections
would suffice to find something coincidental, then *we should* find coincidental
every causal intersection. But it is a fact that this is not the case. Thus, mere

---

[17] Owens, *Causes and Coincidences*, 8.

intersections among independent causal lines are not sufficient to fully determine whether an event is a coincidence or not. There is *something more* in coincidences—something at the mental level—that makes an event a coincidence. With these considerations in place, we now need a closer inspection on what it is this "something more" that is required to properly distinguish between intersections that we find and those that we do not find to be coincidental: our basic insight, here, is to tackle issues concerning our knowledge of these intersections, i.e., *epistemic* features.

Therefore, coincidences are not reducible only to the ontic dimension, which is constituted by the intersection between independent causal lines. They need to involve epistemic features. But how can we think about such features? How exactly do epistemic aspects affect the metaphysical nature of coincidences? To answer this question, let us look at the following distinction made by Richard Rorty:[18]

(1) *Causal* independence: Natural processes and events can exist and operate independently from our minds and will.

(2) *Representational* independence: A privileged vocabulary that lets us pick up things "as they are in themselves", independently from a particular point of view.

We do not have such a super-privileged vocabulary that would enable us to pick up things "as they are in themselves", independent from any point of view. Representing and describing things in one particular way rather than another can strongly modify the way we look at them.

Thus, while intersecting causal lines are causally independent of us, they are *not* representationally independent, and coincidences are *not* representationally independent, either. It appears that our minds are "deciding" and "determining" when and whether certain events are coincidences and when and whether they are not. This approach basically distinguishes between independent intersections that may happen unnoticed from those that can be spotted and appreciated by minded observers. The very concept of coincidence, as we said, involves considerations concerning our interests and perspectives—it directly entails that certain facts and events can be *found to be* coincidental, while others cannot.[19] So, all our grasp of coincidences is connected with the basic fact that

---

[18] Richard Rorty, *Truth and Progress. Philosophical Papers Vol. III* (Cambridge: Cambridge University Press, 1998).

[19] This would also count as an implicit argument for a primacy of epistemological issues over ontic ones, at least in contexts such as this, where epistemic access makes all the difference in the world already in simply conceiving the target of the investigation.

they are not at all independent from our perspectives and representational means.

According to our view, coincidences involve a strong representational dependence: features, abilities, and activities of the subject compose coincidences by representing them as such. Since they involve such mind-dependence, from a metaphysical point of view, coincidences are at least partially mind-dependent events or objects. How do we understand such features?

The Role of Epistemic Access

A first aspect to notice is the following. There could be intersections between independent causal chains that we are not able to recognize because we do not have epistemic access to them. Let us consider Monod's example again: Dr. Dupont is going to visit his patient for the first time. At the same time, in the vicinity, Mr. Dubois is fixing a roof with a hammer. When Dr. Dupont comes across Mr. Dubois' worksite, Mr. Dubois' hammer falls down, and the trajectory of the hammer intersects Dr. Dupont's trajectory. The hammer hits Dr. Dupont's head, causing his sudden death.

First, we should keep firm the trivial, though necessary, statement that only the presence of at least one external observer could acknowledge this event the status of an intersection between independent causal chains. Epistemic access is the filter that permits us to pick up the independent causal sequences setting up the intersection: it is the effective condition needed in order to recognize an intersection as such. Intersections happen, but we need epistemic access in order to identify them. The relevance of this point can be easily underestimated, but ask yourself: Would that intersection count *as a coincidence* in a mindless universe?

So far, we offered an ontic condition about the independence of causal chains, and a general epistemic condition dealing with epistemic access: these are the preliminary basis to a further better understanding of such events.

To conclude, the intersection between independent causal lines, together with the *acknowledgement* of such an intersection, is a requirement for calling an event a coincidence.[20]

The Degree of Epistemic Access

The degree of knowledge that a person could have is very relevant in recognizing the intersection between independent causal chains. Let us consider again Monod's example of Dr. Dupont's death. In that case, if there are no witnesses,

---

[20] However, this requirement alone is not sufficient. See below.

then, of course, it does not make sense to talk about an intersection; but if there are witnesses, the *degree* of knowledge they have is essential. An agent A could see an event E as the result of the intersection between independent causal chains while an agent B does not, because they have a different degree of epistemic access. In order to recognize the ontic layer of coincidences, we need a minimal epistemic perspective in play. Intersections are recognized as such only because we have proper access to them. Appealing to such a role for epistemic access may involve further complications, such as the distinction between ordinary and specialist epistemic access and the justifications that we make for distinguishing different degrees of access. We can imagine, in fact, situations where acknowledging the independence of certain causal chains is open only to a specialist in a particular research or professional field, and the knowledge of ordinary men is not sufficient. Suppose, for example, the case Mr. Dubois is accused of murdering Dr. Dupont. He now seriously risks of being not believed by the judge and convicted of murdering Dr. Dupont. The defence lawyer here has to show the independence between Dr. Dupont's trajectory and Hammer's trajectory, and—in order to do that—he needs to have very specialist and specific knowledge, such as the results of a legal report and so on.

Moreover, the maximum degree of access entails something like a God's eye view, a cosmic exile, or something like that.[21] To claim that a certain causal independence exists in itself, independently of our ken, would count as endorsing an absolute perspective. That perspective is quite hard to endorse since it is external from, more reliable and wider than, our own epistemic stance (and, at least for some, metaphysically extravagant).

Putting aside the controversial issue of absolute perspectives and putative omniscience, we must at least be able to make a distinction, at any rate in principle, between appropriate epistemic access and a poor kind of epistemic access. We need this in order to determine who is right (or wrong) between agent A and agent B, *and to properly understand their disagreement*. The possibility of this difference/disagreement, in fact, is very important for our view, as it can be totally cashed out in terms of epistemic access.

To define a minimum acceptable degree of epistemic access, it is necessary to highlight the features that this kind of access requires:

- A basic conceptual apparatus: the subject must be capable of properly using the concepts "cause", "line", "independence", "intersection", and so on. An epistemic subject without a suitable apparatus can

---

[21] Pierre Simon Laplace, *Essai Philosophique des Probabilités* (Paris: Bachelier, 1814); Willard Van Orman Quine, *Word and Object* (Cambridge, MA: The MIT Press, 1960); Hilary Putnam, *Reason, Truth, History* (Cambridge: Cambridge University Press, 1981).

attend to an intersection without acknowledging that it is made out of independent lines.

- A working perceptual system: the subject must be reliably able to *perceive* two causal lines as intersecting. A subject that cannot see— one that is blind, for example—that the hammer falling down intersects with Dr. Dupont's head cannot realize that it is an intersection of independent causal lines.

- Acknowledgement of the intersection between the independent causal lines, so that the intersection and the independence cannot go unnoticed: the subject must *focus* on them in order to grasp them. This aspect can sometimes be improved, helped, and/or replaced by reliable testimony.

All these conditions entail that any incomplete access is constitutively always inferior to minimal access, where incomplete access indicates a degree of epistemic access that is insufficient to get the relevant facts (about the intersecting lines). This idea of an incomplete access plays a pivotal role in the explanation of the disagreement between agent *A* and agent *B*: *B* has incomplete access to the causal intersection and does not find it coincidental as she fails to notice the independence of the causal sequences that determine the event. Imagine, for example, a variation of Monod's case where we are not allowed to see the intersection under discussion because there is a wall in front of us, and the only thing we see is Mr. Dubois' hammer falling down. As we can easily see, this incomplete access is inferior to any minimal access. We can also imagine this wall as separating two agents (*A* and *B*) and being the source of their disagreement about what is going on: *A* is over the wall and has full perceptual access to the intersection between the hammer and Dr. Dupont; *B* is behind the wall and all she sees is a hammer falling down. The wall here plays the role of an epistemic obstacle, depriving *B* of the very possibility to attend to the causal intersection.

To conclude, the intersection between independent causal lines, together with the acknowledgement of such an intersection and a minimal degree of epistemic access, is necessary for determining whether an event is a coincidence.[22]

Collateral Aspects of the Epistemic Dimension

With all these considerations about the role of the epistemic features in place, it is now possible to raise, in a clear way, a slightly different question: Are there further *non-ontic aspects*, other than epistemic access, that can determine whether an intersection between independent causal lines is a coincidence? Is the "non-ontic" layer of coincidences given entirely in terms of epistemic access?

---

[22] However, these requirements alone are not sufficient. See below.

To answer these questions, it can be useful to consider again, in a more detailed way, Hart and Honoré's definition of a coincidence:

> We speak of a coincidence whenever the conjunction of two or more events in certain spatial or temporal relations is (1) very unlikely by ordinary standards and (2) for some reason significant or important, provided (3) that they occur without any human contrivance and (4) are independent of each other.[23]

According to what Hart and Honoré say regarding point (2), the psychological aspects cannot be removed from the definition of coincidences. This passage from Hart and Honoré, somewhat interestingly, leaving aside the fourth—'independence'—condition, anticipates three epistemic conditions which are quite popular in the literature about epistemic luck: the ways in which it can be fortuitous that some person has a true belief.[24] Condition (1) corresponds to the 'probability/chance' condition—chancy events, just like lucky ones, are understood to be generally not so probable;[25] condition (2) corresponds to the 'significance' condition ("it includes what the agent would find significant were she to be availed of all the relevant facts");[26] and condition (3) corresponds to the 'control' condition: the idea that chancy events escape one's control.

Even though we suppose the "reality" of the absolute independence of intersecting causal lines, and we have (minimal) epistemic access to it, that independence is insufficient to characterize an event as a coincidence. Moreover, minimal access is just a preliminary condition enabling the possibility of triggering conditions (1), (2), and (3) that, given epistemic access to the relevant facts, require that the epistemic subject "judges" what is going on (an intersection of independent causal lines) as not generally *probable, significant* and, at least partly, *out of her control.*

We should fill the global picture with further relevant features.

---

[23] Hart and Honoré, *Causation in the Law,* 74.

[24] However, at this point it is important to specify that this work does not concern epistemic luck, which is a generic notion to describe the ways in which it can be fortuitous that some person has a true belief. Differently, what is discussed here is luck understood as the Aristotelian *autómaton* and *týche.* Both notions are, in fact, very close to the coincidental notion of chance. Aristotle, *Physics, Book II, Chapter V, Paragraph I.*

[25] Duncan Pritchard, *Epistemic Luck* (Oxford: Oxford University Press, 2005), 126; Mylan Engel, "Epistemic Luck", *Internet Encyclopedia of Philosophy,* https://iep.utm.edu/epi-luck/

[26] Pritchard, *Epistemic Luck,* 133.

Attitudes and Beliefs

Condition (2), 'significance', can be grasped more precisely by looking at intentional notions like beliefs, desires and attitudes. Intentionality is usually defined as the capacity of mental states to be about something in the world, e.g., my thought "the President gave a terrible speech yesterday" is about the individual we call "the President" and the words he uttered yesterday. Furthermore, proper intentional states are taken to be contentful, i.e., they bear semantic properties, and can indeed be 'true' or 'false', and also perform other cognitive functions like playing the role of 'premise' or 'conclusion' in inference, and so forth. According to this conception, beliefs, desires, and attitudes, are all about something in the world (comprising also other intentional states), and are all propositionally contentful, and hence we language users are capable to provide explicit (fallible)[27] ascriptions of such states to other people.[28] These basic resources help us refine the understanding of what we mean by "representational" and "perspectival" features concerning the acknowledgment of events as coincidental. The relevance of agents' representational capacities in order to acknowledge coincidences can be approached also the other way around: following a famous and ingenious example from Daniel Dennett, we can imagine Martian super-scientists who can provide complete Laplacian explanations of human behaviour, but who also completely lack intentional notions and ascriptions (the intentional stance). Hence, such Martian super-scientists would be able to predict, by means of a very powerful physical strategy, some human behaviour with great precision. However—given their total lack of intentional notions and ascriptions (i.e., the intentional strategy)— they sometimes would inexorably miss something, ending up in bad bets. As a consequence of that, they would merely see some precise human behaviour as nothing but a random, coincidental, inexplicable fact.[29] According to that view, coincidences are what cannot be explained. However, it remains controversial and to be seen whether one could have explanations at all in a context entirely deprived of intentional states and ascriptions (and the same point holds for coincidences). Hence, as we have already pointed out, we want to discourage this conception and say that intentionality is in place when talking about

---

[27] This fallibility is due to the pervasive phenomenon of the 'intensionality' of intentional ascriptions, i.e., they do not pass the test of substitution *salva veritate* under synonymy. See Pierre Jacob, "Intentionality", *The Stanford Encyclopedia of Philosophy*, 2019, https://plato.stanford.edu/entries/intentionality (section 8).

[28] *Ibid.*

[29] See Daniel Dennett, *The Intentional Stance* (Cambridge, MA: The MIT Press), 25-28.

coincidences. Intentional states play a crucial role in understanding what coincidences are.

Think about the following example from Owens:

> Tomorrow is my wedding day and I crave fine weather, but the forecasters give me little grounds for hope. In desperation I pray for fine weather and, sure enough, tomorrow dawns clear and bright. Those skeptical of the power of the prayer will dismiss this as a coincidence, while many of the faithful will insist it was no coincidence.[30]

Disagreement in belief, in this example, plays a central role in interpreting the event (fine weather during the wedding) as a coincidence or not: a person who believes in the power of prayer would not consider the event a coincidence; conversely, a person who does not believe in the power of prayer would consider the event a coincidence—and naturally they cannot be both right. Therefore, a doxastic difference like having different relevant beliefs is enough to acknowledge the very same event as a coincidence or not (indeed as making a difference for this). So, in a nutshell, beliefs and attitudes can be decisive in the evaluation and acknowledgment of an event as a coincidence.

Here, there is a further relevant factor in play: not only does one need to refuse the belief that the improbable outcome of the weather depends on a kind of divine intervention since that would count—in some sense—as a common cause between the two intersecting causal lines (i.e., my prayer and certain forecast conditions), but the event under discussion must be also *relevant* and *desired* for the agent. Therefore, the causal independence of the causal lines (fine weather, and the hope of fine weather for the wedding day) plus epistemic access to a suitable degree, in this specific case, are *not enough* to establish whether the event is a coincidence or not. That is, the psychological aspects (e.g., beliefs, desires, hopes, and interests) in this context play a very important role in defining the intersection between my prayer and some forecast conditions as a coincidence; this means that the basic elements we tend to consider when we recognize coincidental events are not only the independence between the relevant lines and a certain kind of epistemic access to it. The independence, together with the required degree of epistemic access, are necessary but not sufficient. A certain kind of psychological dependence (what we call the 'significance' condition) is also required, since it is often relevant in classifying an event as a coincidence.

In such a case, believers *do not acknowledge* the coincidence (to them, it is just a prayer answered), while those who are sceptical evaluate the event *as a*

---

[30] Owens, *Causes and Coincidences*, 6.

coincidence.[31] Thus, only having epistemic access to the intersection of causal lines is not sufficient to determine whether it is a coincidence or not. Here, attitudes and beliefs play a role that is independent from simply having access to the intersection. Fine weather is not a coincidence *per se*: we need minded observers who have *not only* epistemic access to the intersection between independent causal lines *but also* relevant attitudes and beliefs in play (e.g., the desire for fine weather, the act of evaluating one type of weather as fine as opposed to others, and so forth). The attitude can work here in a constitutive way; it constitutes the coincidence. This point has interesting consequences because it entails a kind of supremacy of the psychological components (i.e., attitudes and beliefs) over epistemic access when they are relevant in distinguishing whether an intersection is a coincidence or not. In the example from Owens, without the relevant attitudes and beliefs (e.g., without being sceptical about the power of the prayer), there is simply no coincidence at all. Attention, attitudes, values, beliefs, and commitments all can play crucial constitutive roles in *understanding* what we call 'coincidences'. These intentional states and attitudes are able to explain exactly why a particular event can be judged as significant by the agent (and why not when it is not considered significant).

This 'significance' condition can be spelled out also in slightly different terms, for example, in terms of 'relevance'. Although people can see the independence between intersecting causal lines, people can still think that some intersections are not coincidences because the intersections are not, in any sense, relevant. A coincidence is something that is not only unexpected but also relevant to us. This attribution of significance, again, depends on knowledge, beliefs, attitudes, and values, all the doxastic and epistemic components of our mental lives that make a great difference when the moment comes to determine the relevance of something.

Here, relevance is a requirement that is embedded in the epistemic and the psychological sides of our ability to take something as a coincidence. Something is relevant to us because of what we know, what we believe, and what we have been told, but it is also relevant because we like it, love it, or find it desirable, funny, terrible, or any number of other qualities. We often come to know things that catch our interest and tend to ignore things that we find unattractive or boring. Thus, the very fact that we know something cannot be detached *a priori* from our attitudes toward it; a particular attitude can be the very basis of the

---

[31] Also superstition and astrology, being explanations in their own way, rather than providing examples of coincidences, show us that if one believes in some form of explanation, he/she sees far fewer coincidences than those who do not believe. Hence, lack of explanation appears to be a significant requirement for coincidences.

fact that we know something, and it yields the possibility that if we did not like it, we would not know of it. Therefore, it is quite hard to disentangle one aspect from the other since what we know very often depends on what we find interesting, useful, and so on. Vice versa, it happens that we can come to love something only after we know it. There is not a general order to follow: the two aspects are strictly entwined in the realm of "the mental". Relevance is crucial for the acknowledgment of coincidences from many points of view, both from our own personal amount of information and from our personal profile of attitudes. These aspects of relevance are non-negotiable requirements.

Regarding coincidences, relevance/significance can be explained in theoretical (intellectual) and hermeneutic (cultural) terms: 1) the theoretical strategy determines a field of hypothesis, theories, and *specialist* practices where unexpected outcomes—determined by the intersection of independent causal lines—are meaningful, relevant, and interesting as well as surprising and puzzling; 2) the hermeneutic strategy determines a field of beliefs, shared meanings, values, laws, and *ordinary* social practices in which unexpected events—determined by the intersection of independent causal lines—are meaningful, relevant, and interesting as well as surprising and puzzling. Both dimensions are important and decisive since we can distinguish a coincidence that is relevant in a specialist setting from one that is relevant only in ordinary contexts.

Probability

Another point worthy of discussion is what has been called, until now, the unexpected character of coincidences: what we named condition (1), the "chance" condition according to which the relevant event is not a probable one by common standards. The fact that causal sequences interact in a way that is not expected is very important because expectations are mental states characteristic of epistemic subjects. Our best understanding of these expectations is cashed out in terms of subjective probable outcomes of actions and events, and hence it is a matter of subjective probability. Something is generally unexpected when it is unlikely. Our evaluations of probability dealing with what is going on around us determine what is expected and unexpected and what is likely, or very unlikely, to happen.

Indeed, our very ordinary conception of coincidences is strongly affected by our doxastic stance, by what we know, what we believe, and as well by what we expect. As a consequence, we could ask whether a non-unexpected intersection between events that belong to independent causal chains is still a coincidence.

Think about cases in the natural sciences. During a scientist's work in a laboratory, if some causal sequences (e.g., those of two particles) intersect in a way that is expected, even if they are mutually independent from a causal point of view, then what happens is no longer a coincidental event (no chance, no accident, just causal independence). In this case, since a calculation predicts the intersection or at least a hypothesis envisages it, independence is not sufficient to make the intersection a coincidence. That intersection would be a coincidence only if it was something unexpected and not contained in the hypothesis. (It would also be, by the way, an empirical failure for previous false hypotheses.)

This is not anything new, as it is strongly reminiscent of what Aristotle says in *Metaphysics*:

> Going to Aegina was an accident for a man, if he went not in order to get there, but because he was carried out of his way by a storm or captured by pirates. The accident has happened or exists, not in virtue of the subject's nature, however, but of something else; for the storm was the cause of his coming to a place for which he was not sailing, and this was Aegina.[32]

Although the intersection of independent causal lines is a necessary feature for determining coincidences, it is not sufficient since the unexpected component is *always* required. There is an act of judgment, a distinct mental kind of activity, in which we decide whether a particular intersection of causal lines is a coincidental event or not. We may decide that the intersection is a coincidence, or at least we may find it to be so, but a kind of psychological activity regarding the subject is always required.

All this discussion, at this point, allows us to insert this epistemic dimension in a more fine-grained definition of coincidence: a coincidence is an (unexpected) relational event that occurs through the intersection of two or more independent causal sequences. Minded observers must be able to represent the independent causal sequences as coincidental because the observers can recognize their independence; moreover, the act of recognition of coincidences as such involves many other features of our mental activities and certain epistemic conditions: values, beliefs, expectations, attitudes, desires, and whatever can make us see things differently or perceive something as odd or uncommon.

David Hand examined extremely unlikely events, such as coincidences, miracles and so on: not only do events like those occur, according to him, but they keep occurring and are even commonplace.[33] So that, "an inexplicable

---

[32] Aristotle, *Metaphysics, Book V* 1025a, 25-30.

[33] David J. Hand, *The Improbability Principle: Why Coincidences, Miracles, and Rare Events Happen Every Day* (New York: Scientific American/Farrar, Straus and Giroux, 2014).

event (normally a welcome one) attributed to a god: a supernatural event"[34] turns out to be less surprising than some others almost to be expected. In his book, Hand deals with the main reasons for the not-uncommon occurrence of such rarities, stating that events which seem rare, such as the coincidence of my bumping into a falling hammer while going to have a drink with friends, are to be expected. Expected coincidences are not a contradiction in terms, and living organisms also thrive on expected coincidences, anticipating them to survive and flourish. Perhaps what makes a coincidence an "improbable miracle", is that it happens exactly to me, or to a friend of mine, i.e., the fact it is worthy of my particular attention, in a way that one can ask: Why does this good luck or bad luck happen exactly to me? According to our view, a coincidence is not every effect that is brought about by the accidental crossing of independent causal lines: the ordinary man is not bothered by the frequently occurring accidental effects which are not worthy of special note, such as the fact he meets several persons as he walks daily from home to his workplace. But he finds much more worrying about the mysterious occurring meeting between a falling hammer and his friend's head. Coincidences are something that "miraculously" happen to us.

Control

Another important aspect envisaged by Hart and Honoré is that these events somehow "occur without any human contrivance". In the literature, this aspect is employed for defining the concept of epistemic luck—concerning the ways in which it can be lucky/fortuitous that someone has a true belief—and it is usually called the 'control' condition. Very generally, it means that epistemic luck is independent of one's control. Especially, according to Duncan Pritchard, epistemic luck demands *total* independence of one's control:

> Another common way of characterizing luck is in terms of control, or rather the absence of it. If one were to say that, for example, "I discovered the buried treasure by luck", one would be naturally understood as implying that one did nothing to ensure that one discovered what one did—that the discovery itself was out of one's control in some way.[35]

---

[34] Hand, *The Improbability Principle*, 27.

[35] Pritchard, *Epistemic Luck*, 127.

This "control" condition is not a new one. Almost the same can, in fact, be already found in Aristotle and Aquinas, when they teach what it means to state that the same event happens by chance:

> Then, when he [Aristotle] says: It is manifest to me etc., he concludes from the foregoing that concerning the things are simply done for the sake of something, when they do not come to be the cause of what happened to him, but which are made for the sake of anything of external, then we say that they were made by chance.[36]

What exactly is Aquinas, together with Aristotle, saying here?

> Let us consider an agent acting for an end. To say that an agent acts for an end is to say that both the agent and his activity have a determination that comes from that end; it is to say that both the agent and his activity tend toward that end. Now if the agent's activity brings about an event to which he and the activity are not determined; if it brings about something end-like *that is outside the determination of himself and his activity*, we say the agent acted by chance; we say the agent and his activity produced a chance event.[37]

As it can be seen, this passage summed up the same as the "control" condition invoked in the case of epistemic luck. But let us put epistemic luck aside and go back to coincidences.

Think about Monod's example: Dr. Dupont is in control of his walk, he wants to go in a precise direction with a clear aim, that is, visiting a patient. Some kind of control can be involved in one of the relevant causal trajectories. However, Mr. Dubois' hammering is out of Dupont's control, since the two causal histories are mutually independent. Therefore, a form of control is involved, but it is not a control that involves the entire intersection; it can be a kind of control regarding only one of the component causal trajectories. The intersection between Dr. Dupont's walk and Mr. Dubois's hammer is totally *outside the determination* of Dr. Dupont and *his activity*.

The "control" condition, on the basis of Monod's example above, can be refined in teleological terms: Dr. Dupont wants *only* to go to visit his patient and it is not his intention to meet Mr. Dubois' hammer; in the same way, Mr. Dubois wants just to fix the roof and it is not his intention to make the hammer

---

[36] Saint Thomas Aquinas, *Commentary on II Physics, Lect. X* a8. The original in Latin is as follows: «Deinde cum dicit: Quare manifestum est etc., concludit ex praemissis quod in iis quae simpliciter fiunt propter aliquid, quando non fiunt causa eius quod accidit, sed fiunt causa alicuius extrinseci, tunc dicimus quod fiant a casu».

[37] Junkersfeld, *The Aristotelian-Thomistic Concept of Chance*, 41, the italic is our emphasis.

fall down and hit the doctor's head. Dr. Dupont and Mr. Dubois both *do not* intend to produce the tragic accident which instead happens.

Similarly, in *Physics*,[38] Aristotle offers an analysis of chance by means of the following example: a man wants to attain a precise end, that is to watch a play. Hence, he chooses to come to the marketplace, where the theatre is located. Then, he goes to the marketplace, where he unexpectedly encounters his debtor. Thus, he achieves an end *that is outside the determination of himself and his activity:* he collects a debt. According to Aristotle, the man's encounter with the debtor is an outcome of chance, since a chain of causation which is aimed at a particular end, namely to attend a play, brings about an event that it is not intended to produce. In this example, the teleological activity of the man who gets his money back is not intended to get the money back; likewise, the teleological activity of the debtor is not intended to pay the money back.[39]

What about incompetent teleology? Would a failure or success be a coincidence, then? Suppose Mr. Dubois intends to drop a hammer on Dr. Dupont to kill him, but he is not ready in time. Then, in his scramble, he inadvertently kicks another hammer he had not noticed before (killing the doctor). Would this death be a coincidence, then? Following Roderick Chisholm's account[40] of agent-causation, we say that the answer is in the negative. Mr. Dubois has Dr. Dupont's life indirectly in power, that is, there is a sequence of things $<p,..., s>$ such that, starting from his bad intentions, he has p (i.e., his going up to the roof at a certain time) directly in his power, and he has s (i.e., the hammer hitting Dr. Dupont's head and killing him) indirectly in his power. Moreover, the event p is not caused by other events or states of affairs, but it is caused by the agent himself, who causes p in the endeavour to make s happen. So that the man, though by means of the wrong hammer, is responsible for the doctor's death. Suppose once again that Mr. Dubois intends to drop a hammer on Dr. Dupont to kill him, but he is not ready in time. Then, in his scramble, he inadvertently kicks another hammer he had not noticed before. Differently, this time that hammer does not hit and kill the doctor. Would this NON-death be a coincidence, then? Following Chisholm's account, we say that the answer is positive. Mr. Dubois has no power at all in Dr. Dupont's NON-death: the event p (i.e., his going up to the roof at a certain

---

[38] Aristotle, *Physics, Book II* 196b33-197a6, 12-18.

[39] It is important to specify that, although the Aristotelian argument regarding chance is strictly related to the discussion concerning final causes and *telos*, this paper does not engage in a discussion about that.

[40] Roderick Chisholm, "Freedom and Action", in *Freedom and Determinism*, ed. Keith Lehrer (New York: Random House, 1966), 11-44. Reprinted in *The Nature of Human Action*, ed. Myles Brand (Glenview: Scott Foresman and Company, 1970), 283-92.

time) is not caused by other events or states of affairs, but it is caused by the agent himself. However, Mr. Dubois causes p in the endeavour to make the doctor's death happen, which does not happen instead. So that the man is not responsible for the doctor's NON-death. Those examples show once again how the absence of human contrivance is important to define coincidences.

Coincidences, intended as the result of the intersection between independent causal lines, are out of one's control and occur, in some sense, without human contrivance.

In summation, coincidences are as follows:

1. Unexpected—they respect the 'chance' condition

2. Relevant—they respect the 'significance' condition

3. Unplanned (not made by an act of the will)—they respect the 'control' condition

4. Fruits of the intersection between epistemically accessible independent causal lines—they respect the 'ontic independence' condition.

To better clarify our new conception and the different epistemic-psychological aspects at work when determining the occurrence of coincidences, it could be useful to consider the following examples, which sum up the four points just stated.

It is estimated that about six million lightnings strike the ground every day. Kifuka, a village in Congo, is struck every year by almost 158 lightning per square km. In Italy the average is two lightning strikes per square km. The probability of lightning beating a person is much lower. But there is no shortage of very impressive cases of people struck by lightning.

The teenager Ivan Zaborovsky in July 2020 was beaten directly by lightning during a football training session in the Moscow Region. Salaud Akhmatov, a resident of Nazran, Republic of Ingushetia, stepped out onto the balcony of his home in June 2020 during a storm, to watch the flashes in the sky. A lightning hit the glass of the balcony window and passed through his body; the strong shock ripped through his chest, breaking nine ribs. The Italian Simone Toni was struck by a lightning on the Gran Sasso massif during a hike in August 2022; now his friends call him 'Flash'.

In the stunning examples cited, the trajectory of the lightning intercepts the trajectory of the struck person. In the same way, every single day the trajectory of almost six million lightnings intercepts the trajectory of the ground (trees, seas, rivers, and so on).

However, although in both cases there is an intersection of causal chains, only for the first case we speak of coincidences. What is the reason for this difference in interpretation?

Firstly, for most humans it does not matter whether lightnings strike the ground unless that ground is on their property or inside their house and they must fix the damage. Secondly, while it is highly probable that a lightning will strike the ground, it is not equally probable—and then shocking—that lightning will strike a person. Finally, the man's encounter with a lightning is completely out of control, as well as undesirable. The chain of causation, which is aimed at a particular end, for example to watch the storm on the balcony, brings about an event that it is not intended to produce. The teleological activity of the man who gets injured by a lightning is not obviously intended to get that damage.

Conclusion

According to this account, coincidences are complex events for which no single constitutive component is sufficient to warrant their existence:

- Intersections between independent causal lines are necessary for coincidences but are not sufficient without their epistemic acknowledgment, our expectations, our attitudes toward them, and our plans.

- A minimal degree of epistemic access is necessary for coincidences but is not sufficient without the intersection of independent causal lines, as well as certain expectations, beliefs, attitudes, and plans.

- Expectations, beliefs, attitudes and plans are necessary for coincidences but are not sufficient without the intersection between independent causal lines and a certain kind of epistemic access.

The degree of epistemic access plays a very important role in identifying the independence between intersecting causal lines. Moreover, expectations, attitudes, and so on are necessary to define coincidences.

This rich view of the nature of coincidental events directly rules out conceptions like Monod's and Cournot's: strict objectivism about coincidences. The mental (i.e., epistemic and psychological conditions) and the ontic components are both necessary in determining a coincidence, but none is alone sufficient to really understand the nature of coincidences.

Chapter 5

Recent Developments

Some Help from Psychology

This chapter is devoted to introducing some further aspects concerning the psychological dimension of coincidences. We will introduce some new conceptualizations of coincidences and also the results of some empirical research in psychology concerning people's judgments about coincidences, trying to explore those contributions in view of the conceptual tools previously provided. There are, indeed, peculiar facts about how people react when confronted with coincidences, and such facts can be very important to pick up some evidence concerning the features of coincidences that we highlighted so far. On the one hand, these aspects certainly depend on the peculiar psychological conceptions and hypotheses adopted by scholars. On the other hand, empirical research here can offer some clues about our account of coincidences, as we stressed in the previous chapter, that these show important psychological aspects like the fact that they must be generally significant and unlikely to someone.

The first aspect we want to analyse concerns the view according to which coincidences are considered improbable events since this qualification is trickier than it seems (see below). As already illustrated in Chapter 4, according to Hart and Honoré's definition of a coincidence, we speak of a coincidence "whenever the conjunction of two or more events" in some spatial or temporal relations is "very unlikely by ordinary standards".[1] In fact, sometimes some extremely improbable occurrences startle us, and give us stories to tell. Imagine again the scene we introduced in Chapter 2, STORY 1:

> "It was a very springy day and I decided to take a walk in the city centre, where everyone can see colourful balconies of red tulips and yellow daisies. But a tragedy was going to happen: a vase of red tulips fell before my eyes, hitting the head of the man who was walking just few metres ahead. The red of the tulip and the red of his blood mingled like in a huge reddish river. Such bad luck! Such a terrible coincidence!".

This event was certainly unlucky, and even highly improbable: of all the times when the vase could have landed, it just happened to choose that hour, that

---

[1] Hart and Honoré, *Causation in the Law*, 74.

minute and that second framed by the man walking a few metres ahead of me. We know that if someone had tried to throw the vase intending to land in that man's head, he probably would not have succeeded. How could that unlikely event happen? We immediately feel that something mysterious or spooky is going on.

Such an "unlikeliness" requirement for coincidences is strictly related to what we called expectations, i.e., to some mental states which are typical of agents and epistemic subjects, and it can certainly be better understood thanks to some recent research work in psychology. However, this issue in psychology is not entirely new, and many different explanations to those phenomena have been proposed in the past. Among the many, the most popular of them is surely Carl Gustav Jung's synchronicity, which now we will begin to look at briefly as a useful introduction to this topic.

It is necessary to start by saying that, as David Hand nicely points out in his book,[2] expected coincidences are not a contradiction in terms, and that the psychoanalyst Jung thought coincidences occur more frequently than one could explain by chance. Indeed, the big question at the core of his research was: Are coincidences really unlikely events or is this unlikeliness just the fruit of some psychological state?

It was to reply to this question that he was led to develop a theory of synchronicity. In contrast to synchronism, which basically means the simultaneous physical occurrence of two or more events, synchronicity is defined as a coincidence in time of two or more causally unrelated events which have the same or a similar meaning. Think about the following example given by Jung: a young woman he was treating was telling him a dream in which she was giving a golden scarab. Suddenly the psychoanalyst saw in the window of the room a flying insect very similar to a scarab. "Such a coincidence", we would say. As we can easily see, in this example, we have two events that are related in time by a similar meaning: the scarab in the dream and the scarab-looking flying insect. Hence, as the example shows, both the analogous occurrence in time and the presence of a similar meaning are doing the trick here.

Events like those really occur frequently, despite what we usually think. But why are surprising events like those so common? An almost infinite number of events happen all around us all the time; life is just a series of events. For a coincidence, someone must single out events and link them in a meaningful way. Here, the degree of relevance we give to what we are observing drives our

---

[2] Hand, *The Improbability Principle*.

choices: coincidences are so common events because we naturally tend to find a match in the meaning for many things.

Another tentative explanation about why the probability of coincidental events is so high could be "the law of near enough", as Hand calls it. This law says that "events which are sufficiently similar are regarded as identical",[3] such as the scarab in the dream and the scarab-looking flying insect in Jung's example. There is not a perfect match between the first insect and the second one, but—by slightly extending what we mean by a match—it effectively makes it inevitable we discover many coincidences. To regard similar events as identical indefinitely expands the number of potential matches. Hence, given this natural tendency to find matches in meaning, people notice coincidences more and more.

A New Psychological Hypothesis, Empirical Results, and New Conceptual Implications

Now a good question could be the following: Why do we need to find so many coincidences in the world? Again, is there some psychological mechanism that somehow pushes us to see coincidences around? Is this a kind of irrational bias of the human mind that projects connections even where there are none? A very inspiring work in this respect comes from cognitive psychologists Mark K. Johansen and Magda Osman, who—in their *Coincidences: A fundamental consequence of rational cognition*—argue that the experience of coincidences is a necessary consequence of rational causal learning mechanisms, rather than just being examples of irrationality.[4]

As Johansen and Osman highlight, the main idea is that people use "the same properties relevant for causal reasoning" when "detecting and evaluating events" that are ultimately judged to be coincidences.[5] So, their idea is that whenever a judgment about something coincidental is going on, people rely on properties and features that are usually relevant for causal reasoning. If this hypothesis holds, it could dismiss usual common-sense views that typically present such judgments as simply irrational, such as biased probabilistic reasoning or paranormal beliefs.[6] Coincidences, according to Johansen and Osman's

---

[3] Hand, *The Improbability Principle*, 201.

[4] Johansen and Osman, "Coincidences: A fundamental consequence of rational cognition", 34-44. This idea can in principle explain the aforementioned tendency to find matches in meaning. It would be just a phenomenon connected with our dispositions to explain events in a causal way (see below).

[5] Johansen and Osman, "Coincidences: A fundamental consequence of rational cognition", 34.

[6] Johansen and Osman, "Coincidences: A fundamental consequence of rational cognition", 35.

view, are just an unavoidable feature of the human mind "searching for causal structure in reality". [7] Coincidences, from this point of view, are just phenomena deeply connected with how the human mind perceives events going on in the surroundings, along with a tendency to highlight possible causal explanations. It all depends, at the end of the day, on mechanisms for inferring causality in what is going on. According to them, coincidences are "surprising pattern repetitions" that are observed to be unlikely by ordinary standards but are nonetheless attributed to chance as our attempts at causal explanation have not produced "anything more plausible than mere chance". [8]

This diagnosis sits at the base of their view about the cognitive mechanism that we exploit when we acknowledge a particular event as a coincidence. This view goes under the name of "the 3 C's framework" for coincidences. [9] The 3 C's stand for the three distinct phases of the cognitive mechanism: first of all, there is a stage where subjects enact the detection of a particular pattern repetition that is considered somehow surprising or unlikely; then there is the second stage in which subjects look for possible explanations of that coincidence; and then there is the third stage, in which the merits of a coincidental interpretation and those of a causal interpretation are compared and valued in terms of probability, in order to understand if the coincidence can be explained away by some relevant cause. When the causal interpretation is untenable, we must resort to invoking a coincidence.

Look at the following example: suppose I am going to the beach in the sea city where I live in Sardinia. During my walk, I meet a guy who was my neighbour where I used to live in the USA, that is on the opposite side of the world; and suppose it has been something like ten years I have not seen him and kept in touch with him. Such a surprising event! Then, suppose after two months, I decide to have a trip to Ireland, to visit the Cliffs of Moher, and there I meet once more time my American neighbour. What if I would keep on meeting him again and again in different places within a short time? That would be a very surprising and unlikely pattern repetition. I would try for sure to give a causal explanation, especially because I am not superstitious, and I do not believe in any God's plan. However, given the fact I do not find any plausible causal explanation, I conclude that the surprising meetings were produced by nothing but mere chance.

---

[7] *Ibid.* In this sense, the idea that the human mind looks for causal structure is basically the explanation for our need to find matches in meaning about what takes place around us.

[8] Johansen and Osman, "Coincidences: A fundamental consequence of rational cognition", 36.

[9] Johansen and Osman, "Coincidences: A fundamental consequence of rational cognition", 39.

As the example shows, coincidence is generally accepted in those cases in which the causal alternative explanations do not work in providing a better account, or are simply unavailable. This means that the search for plausible causal mechanisms underlying the relevant happenings/events continues in an attempt to lighten "the surprisingness" of the putative coincidence. So, according to this framework, subjects tend to judge that a particular event *E* is a coincidence if and only if they lack a better/tenable causal alternative. This framework, furthermore, is especially useful in producing a new definition of coincidences: according to Johansen and Osman, these are surprising pattern repetitions that are observed to be "unlikely by chance" but are nonetheless attributed to chance since the search for causal explanations has not yielded any plausible candidates.[10] People recognize an event as a coincidence when they clearly lack a plausible causal explanation of what is going on.[11]

Johansen and Osman, in a second moment, exploited this framework as the conceptual basis to perform some psychological experiments concerning the question "how coincidental is this?" in order to measure people's reactions

---

[10] *Ibid.* This definition is quite in line with ours and with the intersectionist tradition, as the difficulty in finding any plausible causal explanation is accounted for in terms of the mutual independence of the relevant causal chains. Causal explanation fails because there is this independence.

[11] According to this conception, coincidences assume explanatory relevance, i.e., they are inserted in those attempts intended to characterize the relationship that exists between the phenomenon to be explained (*explanandum*) and what explains it (*explanans*). More precisely, according to Johansen and Osman, cognitive agents determine, through motivations, beliefs, and information they possess, the type of explanation required for understanding a given phenomenon. Therefore, the explanatory role of coincidences here assumes a highly pragmatic nature. The traditionally most affirmed and discussed pragmatic theory of explanation is Bas van Fraassen's *Why-questions* theory: according to it, an explanation is simply an answer to a question-Why. This theory has in a certain sense supplanted the theories according to which there is a close link between causality and explanation, already present in the Aristotelian theory of causes, but criticized by the Humean argument which states that causal links are not present in our experience, and criticized by the logical empiricism. Van Fraassen, with his constructive empiricism, identifies scientific practice with an activity of construction rather than discovery, reproposing some fundamental positivist principles, but avoiding however the most implausible aspects of that philosophical view. For a more detailed discussion on this particular issue, the reader may refer to Bas van Fraassen, *The Scientific Image* (Oxford: University Press, 1980); Philip Kitcher and Wesley Salmon, "Van Fraassen on Explanation", *Journal of Philosophy* 84, no. 6 (1987): 315; Alan Garfinkel, *Forms of Explanation. Rethinking the Questions in Social Theories* (New Haven, CT: Yale University Press 1981).

when confronted with coincidences.[12] A preliminary aspect of such experiments concerns the development of a formal model to predict coincidence judgment: so far, in fact, scholars' attention in this field has been mainly devoted to developing formal methods just capable of predicting causal reasoning.[13] Their experiments have been also capable of proving that causal conclusions, as such, always involve a decision between cause and coincidence.[14] More in general, these experiments showed that there is a tight relationship between causal discovery and coincidence perception, and this basically confirms the goodness of their hypothesis about a structural connection between causal reasoning and coincidence. This connection is the mechanism that plays the starring role, in fact, also in judgments about how coincidental can be a particular event.

Their experiments showed that, in general, what they call 'coincidentality'— people's general willingness to make assertions about coincidences—is a rather "stable psychological construct" with important degrees of "agreement between participants and experiments" especially in terms of "correspondence with other psychological judgment variables".[15] This is an empirical evidence showing, among many things, that psychological phenomena are especially relevant when coincidental events are at stake, and we welcome such evidence as lending new support to our hybrid view in which such aspects are explicitly recognized as determining factors.

So far, we have explained why coincidences are so common, but what makes coincidences unlikely? As already told in the previous chapter, perhaps what makes a coincidence an "improbable miracle", is that it happens exactly to me, or to a friend of mine, i.e., the fact it is worthy of my particular attention, in a way that one can ask: Why does this good luck or bad luck happen exactly to me? Following Johansen and Osman's work, people's evaluation of coincidences is influenced by a variety of judgment biases, especially in terms of probability estimation. The most notable bias in the vicinity seems to be the "egocentric one", in which people tend to give higher estimates of rarity and surprise to

---

[12] Johansen and Osman, "Coincidental Judgment in Causal Reasoning: How Coincidental is This?"

[13] Johansen and Osman, "Coincidental Judgment in Causal Reasoning: How Coincidental is This?", 2.

[14] Johansen and Osman, "Coincidental Judgment in Causal Reasoning: How Coincidental is This?", 17.

[15] *Ibid.* Their research also highlighted the need for the deployment of a better "normative conceptualization" of coincidence evaluation as a constitutive part of causal reasoning/ discovery. So, these empirical results still have some limits and need further improvements and conceptual refinements.

personally experienced coincidences than to those experienced by others.[16] This bias seems responsible for accounting for *different* judgments about *similar* probability estimates: these estimates change as far as personal experiences and/or acquaintances are involved. Vice versa, it means that people are generally more realistic and reliable in such estimates when they are not personally involved in what is to be judged.[17]

Moreover, according to our view, a coincidence is not every effect that is brought about by the accidental crossing of independent causal lines: the ordinary man is not bothered by the frequently occurring accidental effects which are not worthy of special note, such as the fact he meets several persons as he walks daily from home to his workplace. But he finds much more worrying the mysterious occurring meeting between a falling hammer and his friend's head. As Johansen and Osman state, it probably happens because the meaningfulness of the coincidence is closely tied to the egocentric bias. In fact, meaningfulness is related to the importance of personally relevant causal mechanisms, especially in terms of usefulness. Hence, it is generally more important for a person to detect potential causes impinging on her than that another man reports as impinging on him.[18] So, it is generally more important to escape a falling hammer that is falling in my head than one falling in yours! Coincidences are something that "miraculously" happen to us as they involve something that we deem important for us, and the egocentric bias seems to play an important role in that.

We can conclude that coincidental events are not just generically unlikely, but they occur much more frequently than we usually think, and this is for the psychological reasons we talked about above. We can even say that, for other psychological reasons, we tend to consider coincidences, as very improbable events (as highlighted in Chapter 4). This is for sure because probability is not, in the case of coincidences, a physical property but it is just a subjective and a psychological one.[19] So, at the end of the day, not only are psychological

---

[16] Johansen and Osman, "Coincidences: A Fundamental Consequence of Rational Cognition", 42.

[17] This aspect, by the way, should be handled with care: if coincidences figure in first-person reports *in controversial cases*, this fact could indicate plausible grounds to raise the egocentric bias' objection against the authenticity of the reported coincidence (i.e., a legitimate suspicion according to which there is no coincidence, but just the bias).

[18] Johansen and Osman, "Coincidences: A fundamental Consequence of Rational Cognition", 42.

[19] With this we do not want to say that psychological probability does not belong to the physical world or is in principle unexplainable in physical terms. We are just saying that it entails a convenient use of psychological resources and other resources coming from

features to be inserted in our general understanding of coincidences, but they can also be used in accounting for the differences in judgments that we may encounter when talking about a certain coincidence with other people. Hence, this is quite telling about certain examples that we presented in Chapter 4, such as Owens' short story about the wedding and the fine weather: believers and non-believers in the power of prayers disagree whether there is a coincidence or not going on in that fictional episode. Now we can add that this special difference can be illuminated by the presence of the egocentric bias: "my" beliefs here can make all the difference in the world in making judgments and estimates about something being a coincidence. So, a general moral that we can extract from this final incursion in recent psychological work can be seen as a general external confirmation that the independence of the causal lines involved in a coincidental event, even though necessary, is alone insufficient to provide a full and proper understanding of the occurring circumstance. Epistemic and psychological features play a major role: intersections of causal processes happen around us all the time, but we do not see them all as coincidences. We just see as coincidences those that are significant.

Psychological Research and Our Hybrid View

Our hybrid conception of coincidences presented in Chapter 4—inspired by the work of Hart and Honoré—can be, once again, summarised as follows:

> Coincidences are unexpected—they respect what we called the 'chance' condition. They are relevant for us—they respect what we called the 'significance' condition. They are unplanned (not made by an act of the will)—that is, they respect what we called the 'control' condition. And, finally, they are also fruits of the intersection between epistemically accessible independent causal lines—they respect what we called the 'ontic independence' condition.

This summary of our view on coincidences can be read in a slightly refined way thanks to the findings in recent psychological research that we highlighted in the preceding sections.

First of all, we detect coincidences in a very particular situation, as highlighted by Johansen and Osman: that is, we acknowledge them in the context of attempting to explain what is going on around us in a causal way. What we called the 'unexpected' aspect of coincidences surely finds here its underlying rationale:

---

subjective probability. Physical explanation here, from the point of view of our current knowledge, simply is not illuminating and would require many successful reductions of the subjective elements to the physical that are still to be provided.

we find them unexpected because we usually acknowledge regular patterns and general regularities in our efforts to causally explain all the happenings around us. We are struck by the breaking up of these typical causal regularities. What we called the 'chance' condition is triggered by our surprising failure in our attempts at causal explanation.

Second, this feature is the basis of the surprisingness of coincidences, which is especially important in understanding why they are so significant for us: they are special, significant, and ultimately surprising insofar as they violate the regular patterns of the causal explanation of the phenomena usually happening around us. What we called the 'significance' condition is triggered by the fact that the causal explanation here fails in an unexpected way, with results that significantly differ from regular casual patterns in everyday experience.

Third, Johansen and Osman pointed out the fact that there is always a choice at stake in the evaluation of an event, especially a choice between two possible outcomes of the evaluation: either it is something causally explainable, or it is a coincidence. We reach the latter verdict when there is evidence that causal explanation fails and it is clearly insufficient to account for the special phenomenon under scrutiny.

All these aspects are also perfectly in line with what we called the 'control' condition, that is, the fact that the phenomenon under scrutiny is not subject to our control—as we humans are especially interested in the facts that are not under our control. These aspects, finally, implicitly align with the last condition that we highlighted, that is with the 'ontic independence' condition: the fact that coincidences are determined by the intersection between independent causal trajectories explains why our causal explanation fails, resulting in our significant surprise and determining our choice to declare it a coincidence.

References

Armstrong, David M. *A World of States of Affairs*. Cambridge: Cambridge University Press, 1997.

Beebee, Helen. "Causing and Nothingness". In *Causation and Counterfactuals*, edited by John Collins, Ned Hall, and Laurie A. Paul, 291-308. Cambridge, MA: MIT Press, 2004.

Chisholm, Roderick. "Freedom and Action". In *Freedom and Determinism*, edited by Keith Lehrer, 11-44. New York: Random House, 1966. (Reprinted in *The Nature of Human Action*, edited by Myles N. Brand, 283-292. Glenview: Scott Foresman and Company, 1970).

Collingwood, Robin George. *An Essay in Metaphysics*. Oxford: Oxford University Press, 1940.

Collins, John, Ned Hall, and Laurie A. Paul, eds. *Causation and Counterfactuals*. Cambridge, MA: MIT Press, 2004.

Cournot, Antoine Augustine. *Exposition de la Théorie des Chances et des Probabilités*. Paris: Hachette, 1843.

Cournot, Antoine Augustine. *Essai sur les Fondements de nos Connaissances et sur les Caractères de la Critique Philosophique*. Paris: Hachette, 1851.

Cournot, Antoine Augustine. *Traité de l'Enchaînement des Idées Fondamentales dans les Sciences et dans l'Histoire*. Paris: Hachette, 1861.

Dennett, Daniel C. *The Intentional Stance*. Cambridge MA: The MIT Press, 1987.

Engel, Mylan. "Epistemic Luck". *Internet Encyclopedia of Philosophy*, 2011. http://www.iep.utm.edu/epi-luck/

Gallow, J. Dmitri. "The Metaphysics of Causation". *The Stanford Encyclopedia of Philosophy*, 2022. https://plato.stanford.edu/entries/causation-metaphysics/

Garfinkel, Alan. *Forms of Explanation. Rethinking the Questions in Social Theories*. New Haven, CT: Yale University Press 1981.

Gasking, Douglas. "Causation and Recipes". *Mind* 64, no. 256 (1955): 479-87.

Hájek, Alan "The Interpretations of Probability". *The Stanford Encyclopedia of Philosophy*, 2019. https://plato.stanford.edu/entries/probability-interpret/#MaiInt

Hand, David J. *The Improbability Principle: Why Coincidences, Miracles, and Rare Events Happen Every Day*. New York: Scientific American/Farrar, Straus and Giroux, 2014.

Hart, Herbert Lionel Adolphus and Anthony Honoré. *Causation in the Law*. Oxford: Clarendon Press, 1959.

Hume, David. *An Inquiry Concerning Human Understanding*. New York: The Bobbs-Merrill Co., 1955[1740].

Hume, David. *Treatise of Human Nature*. Oxford: Clarendon Press, 1888 [1739-40].

Hutto, Daniel and Erik Myin. *Radicalizing Enactivism. Basic Minds without Content*. Cambridge MA: The MIT Press, 2013.

Jacob, Pierre. "Intentionality". *The Stanford Encyclopedia of Philosophy*, 2019. https://plato.stanford.edu/entries/intentionality/

Johansen, Mark K. and Magda Osman. "Coincidences: A Fundamental Consequence of Rational Cognition". *New Ideas in Psychology* 39, 2015. https://doi.org/10.1016/j.newideapsych.2015.07.001

Johansen, Mark K. and Osman, Magda. "Coincidental Judgement in Causal Reasoning: How Coincidental is This?" *Cognitive Psychology* 120, 2020. https://doi.org/10.1016/j.cogpsych.2020.101290

Junkersfeld, M. Julienne. *The Aristotelian-Thomistic Concept of Chance*. Notre Dame: University of Notre Dame, 1945.

Kitcher, Philip and Salmon, Wesley. "Van Fraassen on Explanation". *Journal of Philosophy* 84, no. 6 (1987): 315-30.

Lando, Tamar. "Coincidence and Common Cause". *Noûs* 51, no. 1 (2017): 132-51. doi: 10.1111/nous.12166

Lange, Marc. *Laws and Lawmakers. Science, Metaphysics, and the Laws of Nature*. Oxford: Oxford University Press, 2009.

Laplace, Pierre Simon. *Essai Philosophique des Probabilités*. Paris: Bachelier, 1814.

La Placette, Jean. *Traité des Jeux de Hasard, Défendus Contre les Objections de M. de Joncourt et de Quelques Autres*. La Haye: Chez Henry Scheurleer, Marchand Libraire prés de la Cour, à l'Enfeigne d'Erafme, 1714.

Lewis, David K. *Philosophical Papers. Vol. II*. Oxford: Oxford University Press, 1987.

Martin, Thierry. *Probabilités et Critique Philosophique selon Cournot*. Paris: Vrin, 1996.

Melas, Alessandra. "An Ontic conception of chance in Monod's Non-Teleological Evolutionary Biological Theory". In *An Anthology of Philosophical Studies Volume 9*, edited by Patricia Hanna, 71-86. Athens: Athens Institute of Education and Research, 2015.

Melas, Alessandra. "Cournot's Notion of Hasard: an Objective Conception of Chance". *Axiomathes* 27, no. 6 (2017): 685-697. https://doi.org/10.1007/s105 16-017-9333-7

Melas, Alessandra and Salis, Pietro. "On the Nature of Coincidental Events". *Axiomathes* 32, no. 1 (2022):143-168. https://doi.org/10.1007/s10516-020-09517-4

Menzies, Peter and Price, Huw. "Causation as a Secondary Quality". *British Journal for the Philosophy of Science* 44, no. 2 (1993): 187-203.

Menzies, Peter. "Causation in Context". In *Causation, Physics, and the Constitution of Reality*, edited by Huw Price and Richard Corry, 191-223. Oxford: Oxford University Press, 2007.

Monod, Jacques. *Le Hasard et la Nécessité: Essai sur la Philosophie Naturelle de la Biologie Moderne*. Paris: Éditions du Seuil, 1970.

Monod, Jacques. *Chance and Necessity: Essay on the Natural Philosophy of Modern Biology*. New York: Vintage, 1971.

Moore, Michael S. *Causation and Responsibility: An Essay in Law, Morals, and Metaphysics*. Oxford: Oxford University Press, 2009. doi:10.1093/acprof:oso/9780199256860.001.0001

Noordhof, Paul. "Probabilistic Causation, Preemption, and Counterfactuals". *Mind* 108, no. 429 (1999): 95-125.

Owens, David. *Causes and Coincidences*. Cambridge: Cambridge University Press, 1992.

Pearl, Judea. *Causality*. New York: Cambridge University Press, 2000.

Poincaré, Henri. *Calcul des Probabilités*. Paris: Gauthier-Villars, Imprimeur-Libraire, 1912.

Price, Huw. "Causation, Intervention, and Agency: Woodward on Menzies and Price". In *Making a Difference: Essays on the Philosophy of Causation*, edited by Helen Beebee, Christopher Hitchcock, and Huw Price. Oxford: Oxford University Press, 2017.

Price, Huw and Richard Corry, eds. *Causation, Physics, and the Constitution of Reality*. Oxford: Oxford University Press, 2007.

Pritchard, Duncan. *Epistemic Luck*. Oxford: Oxford University Press, 2005.

Putnam, Hilary. *Reason, Truth, History*. Cambridge: Cambridge University Press, 1981.

Quine, Willard Van Orman. *Word and Object*. Cambridge MA: The MIT Press, 1960.

Reichenbach, Hans. *The Direction of Time*. Dover: University of California Press, 1956.

Rorty, Richard. *Truth and Progress. Philosophical Papers Vol III*. Cambridge: Cambridge University Press, 1998.

Salmon, Wesley. *Scientific Explanation and the Causal Structure of the World*. Princeton: Princeton University Press, 1984.

Sellars, Wilfrid. *Empiricism and the Philosophy of Mind*. Cambridge MA: Harvard University Press, 1997 [1956].

Suppes, Patrick, *A Probabilistic Theory of Causality*. Amsterdam: North-Holland Publishing, 1970.

Thomson, Judith Jarvis. "Causation: Omissions". *Philosophy and Phenomenological Research* 66, no. 1 (2003): 81-103. doi:10.1111/j.1933-1592.2003.tb00244.x

Van Fraassen, Bastiaan Cornelis. *The Scientific Image*. Oxford: University Press, 1980.

Varzi, Achille. *Ontologia*. Roma-Bari: Laterza, 2005.

Vidunas, Raimundas. "Delegated Causality of Complex Systems". *Axiomathes* 29, no. 1 (2019): 81-97. https://doi.org/10.1007/s10516-018-9377-3

Von Wright, George. *Causality and Determinism*. New York: Columbia University Press, 1975.

Woodward, James. *Making Things Happen: A Theory of Causal Explanation*. Oxford: Oxford University Press, 2003.

Woodward, James. "Causation and Manipulability". *The Stanford Encyclopedia of Philosophy*, 2016. https://plato.stanford.edu/entries/causation-mani/

Index

T

U

V

W

www.ingramcontent.com/pod-product-compliance
Lightning Source LLC
Chambersburg PA
CBHW071058280326
41928CB00050B/2553